BUTTERFLIES and FLOWERS

Coloring book

50 Enchanting Grayscale Drawings for Adults Looking
for Relaxation & Stress Relief

by

Diana Tesauro

"The purest and most thoughtful minds are those that love colors."

John Ruskin

Informative notes::

- Please note that using wet media such as markers, fineliners, etc., on this type of paper may result in unintended effects such as smudging, bleeding, or ink transfer onto the next page. To achieve optimal results and preserve the integrity of your artwork, it is recommended to use dry media tools such as colored pencils, pastels, etc. The inclusion of dark backgrounds behind each design serves the specific purpose of providing a layer of protection between pages, thus reducing the likelihood of unwanted smudging or color transfer onto the next drawing;

Thank you for your attention and understanding.

Happy creating!

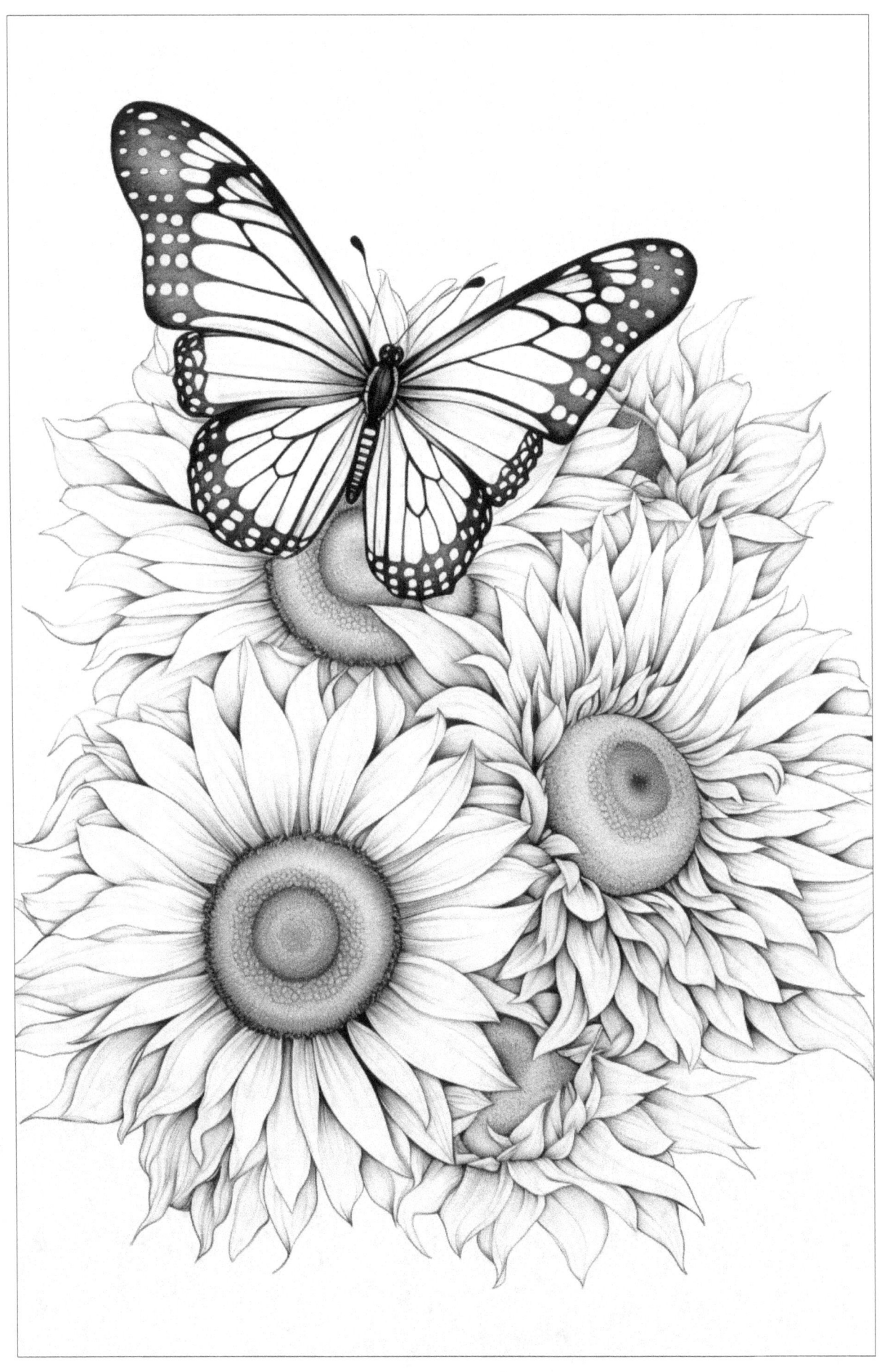

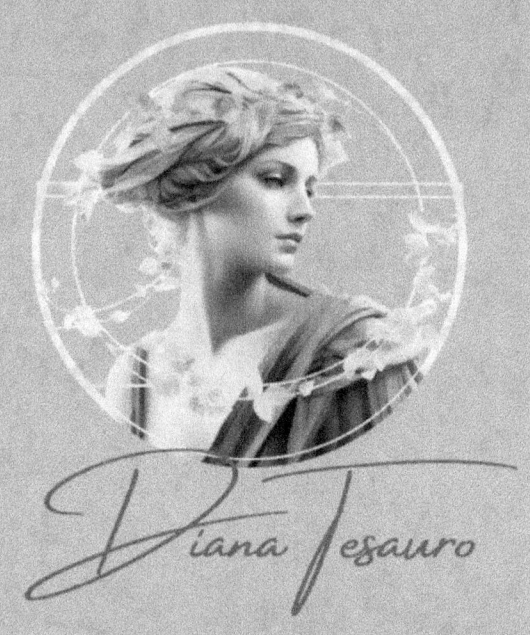

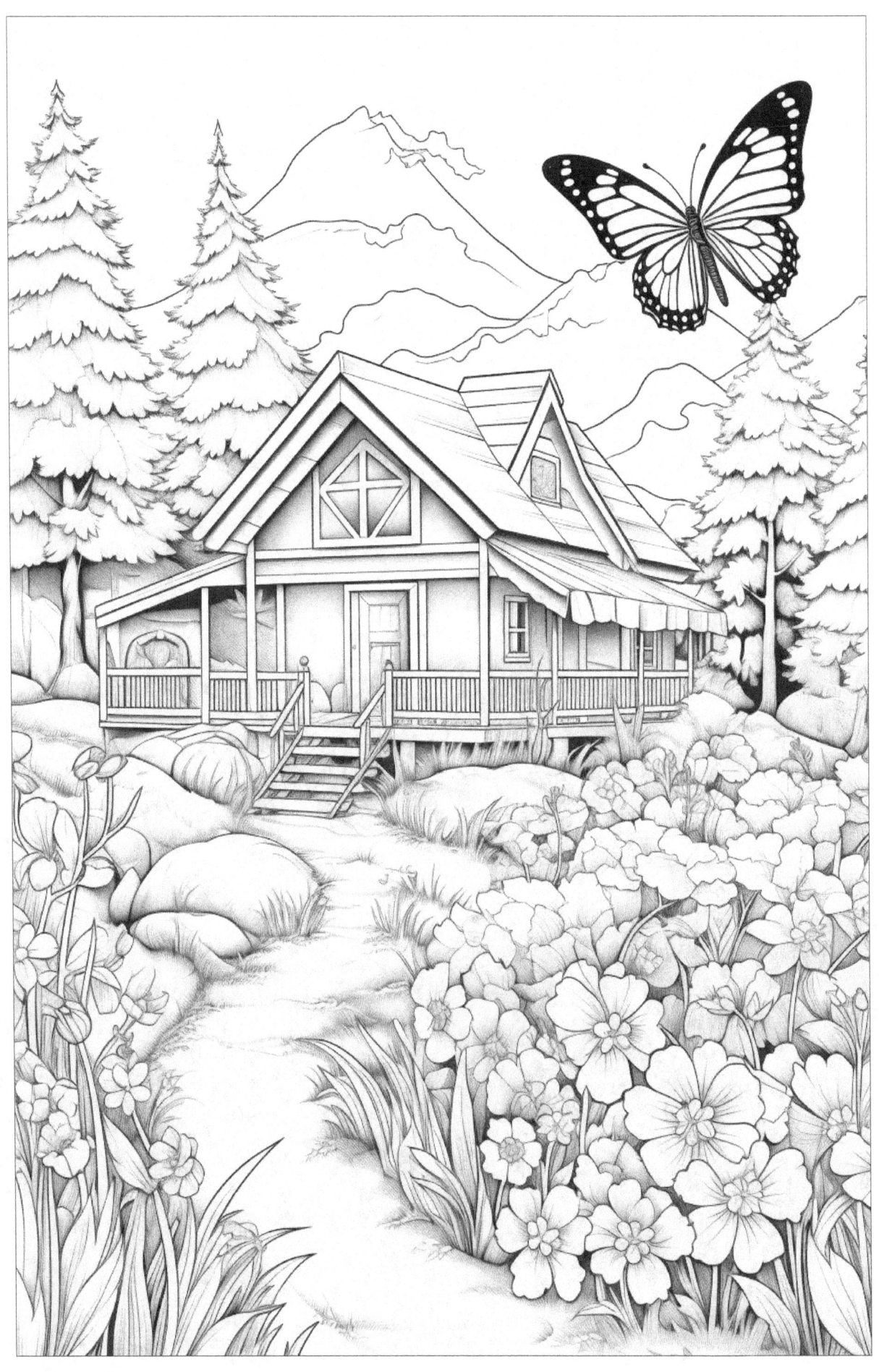

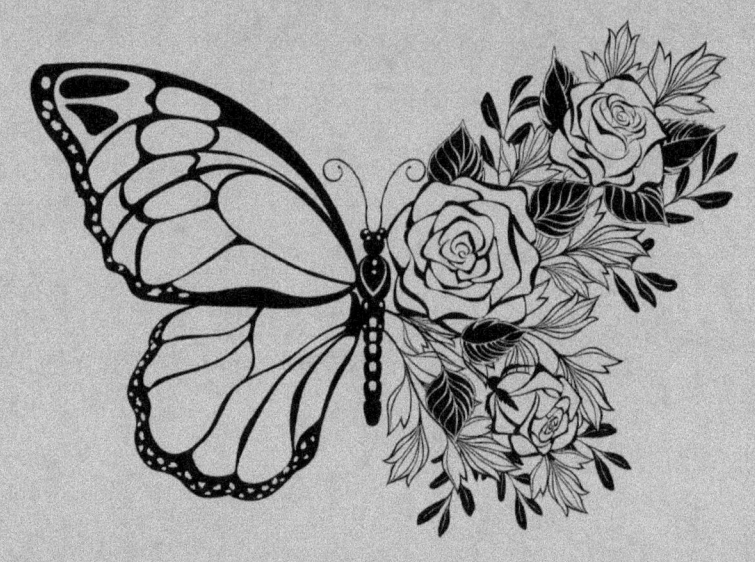

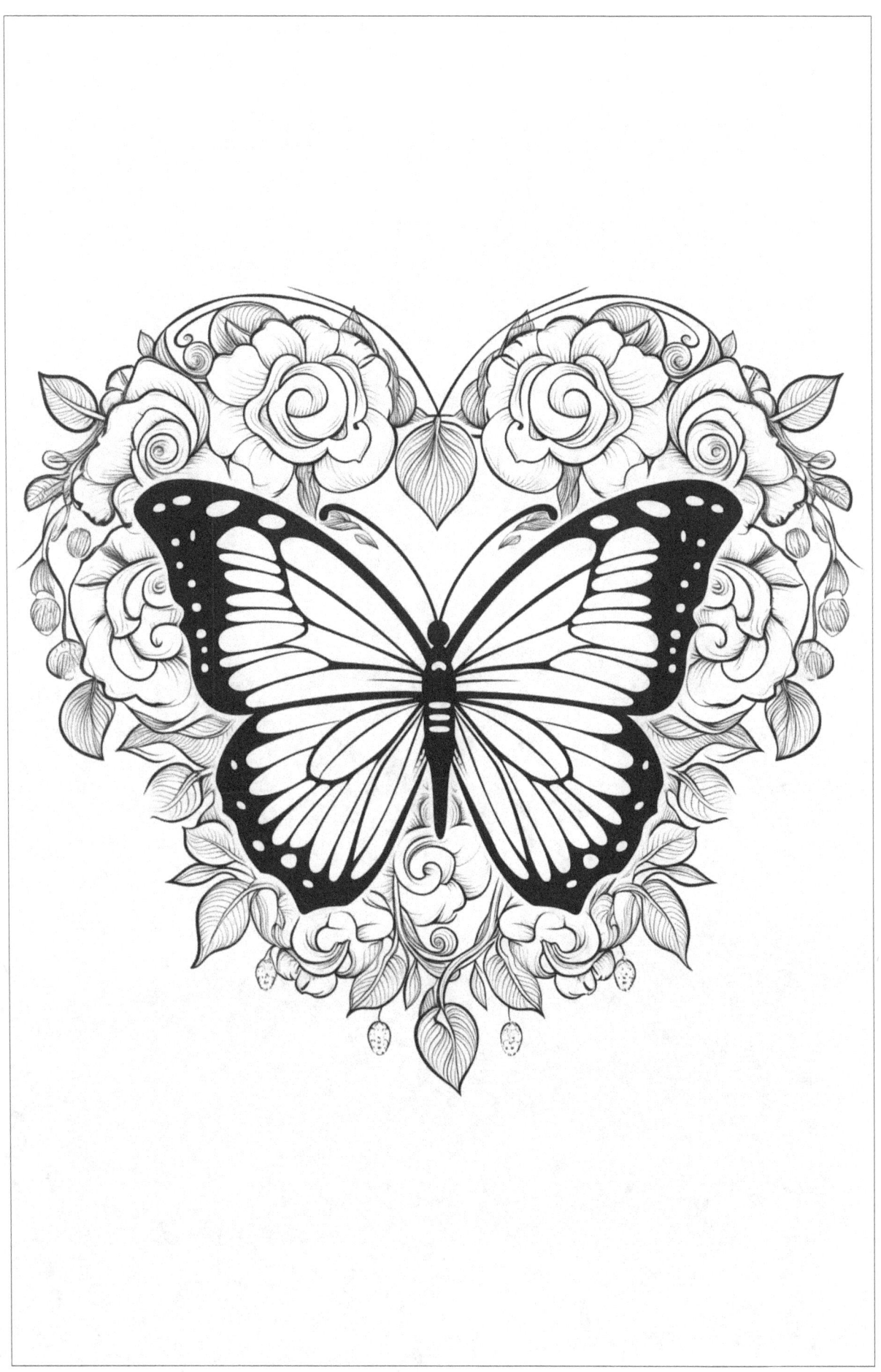

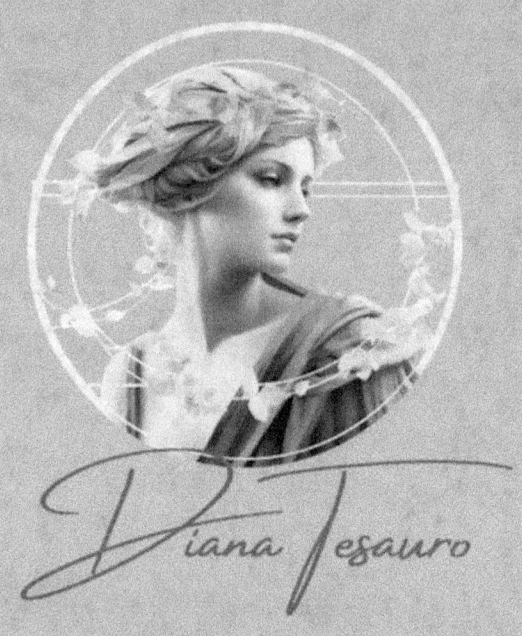

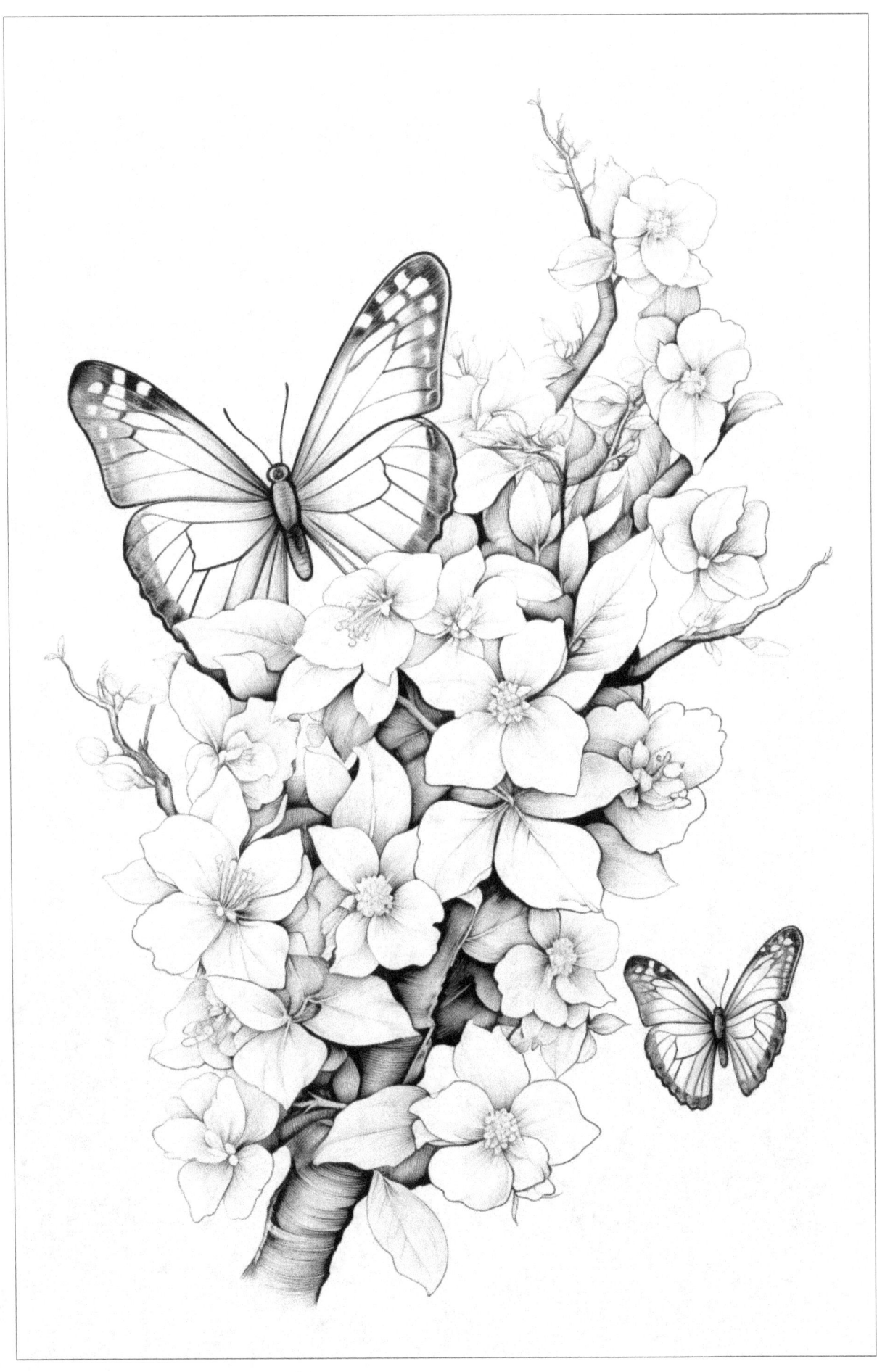

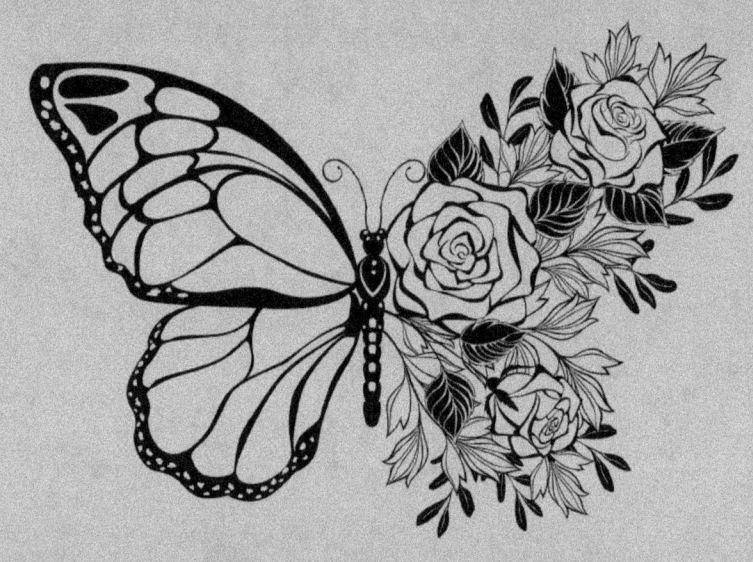

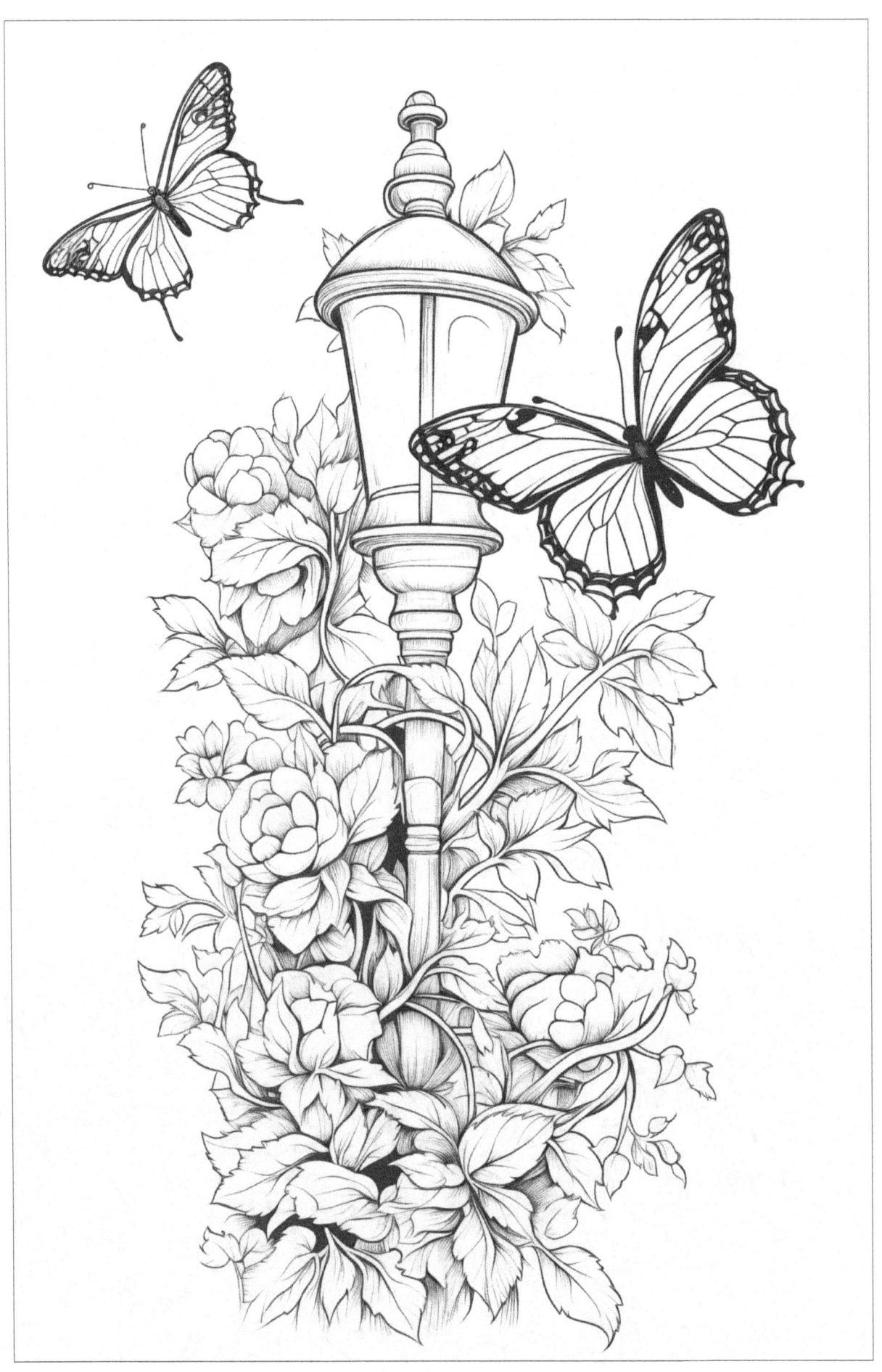

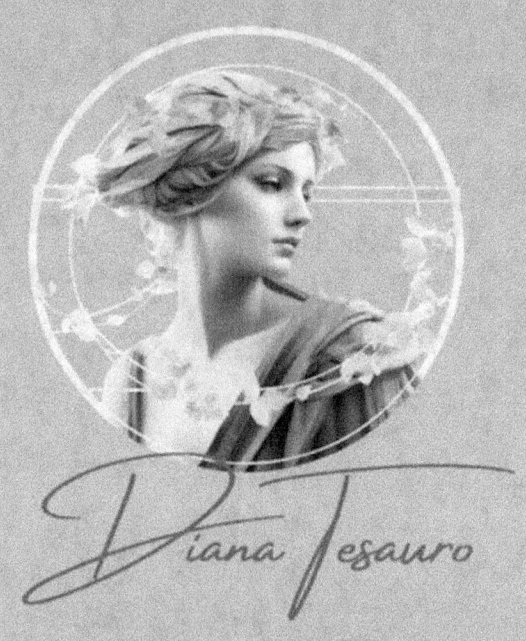

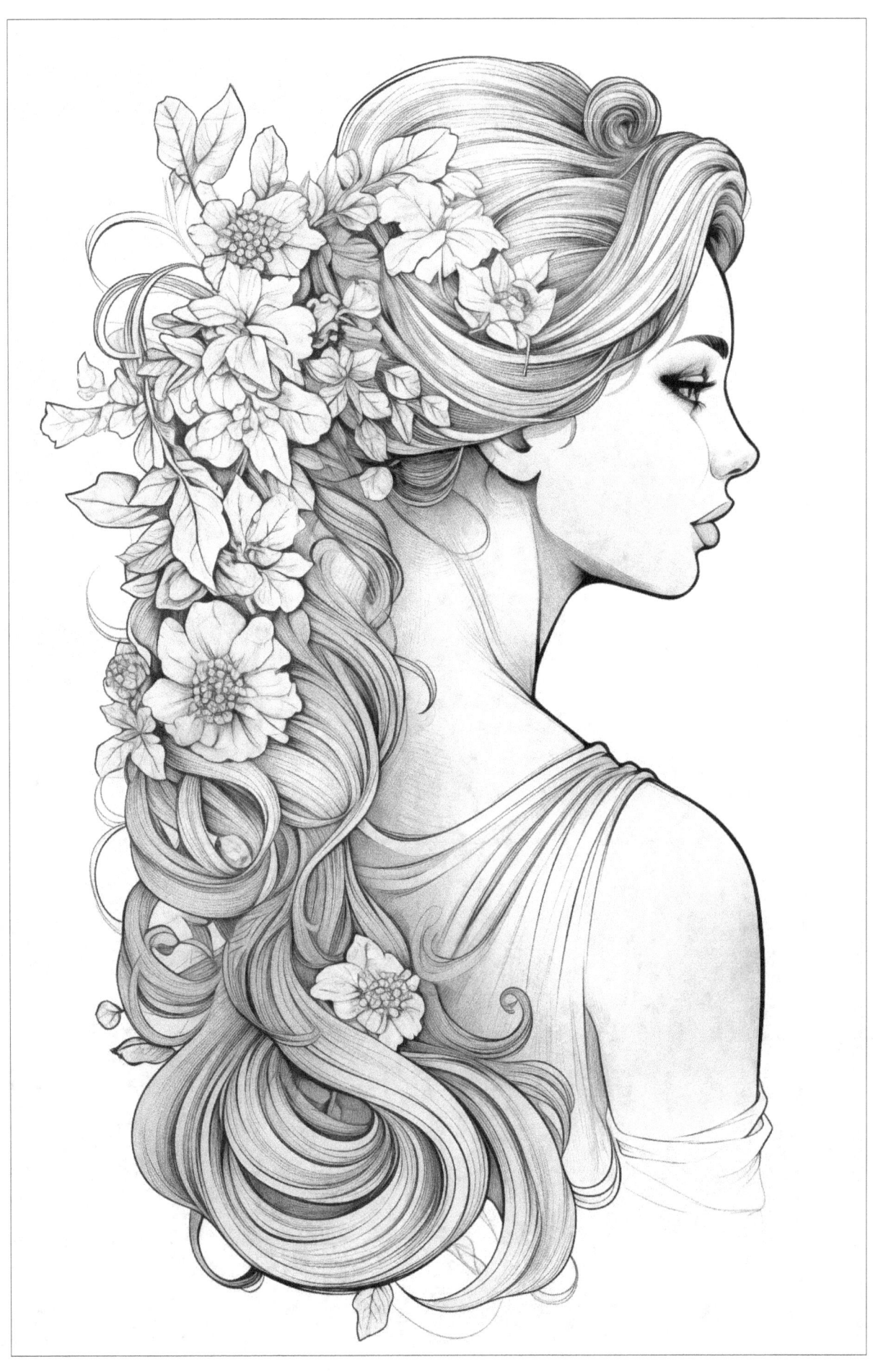

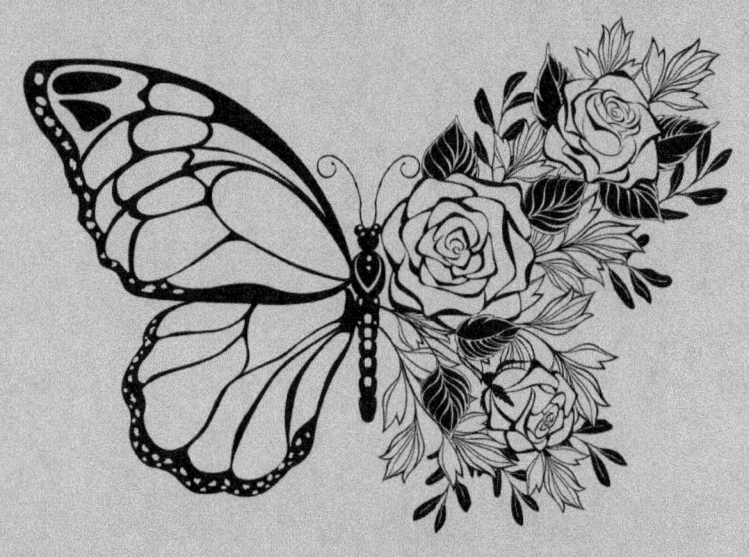

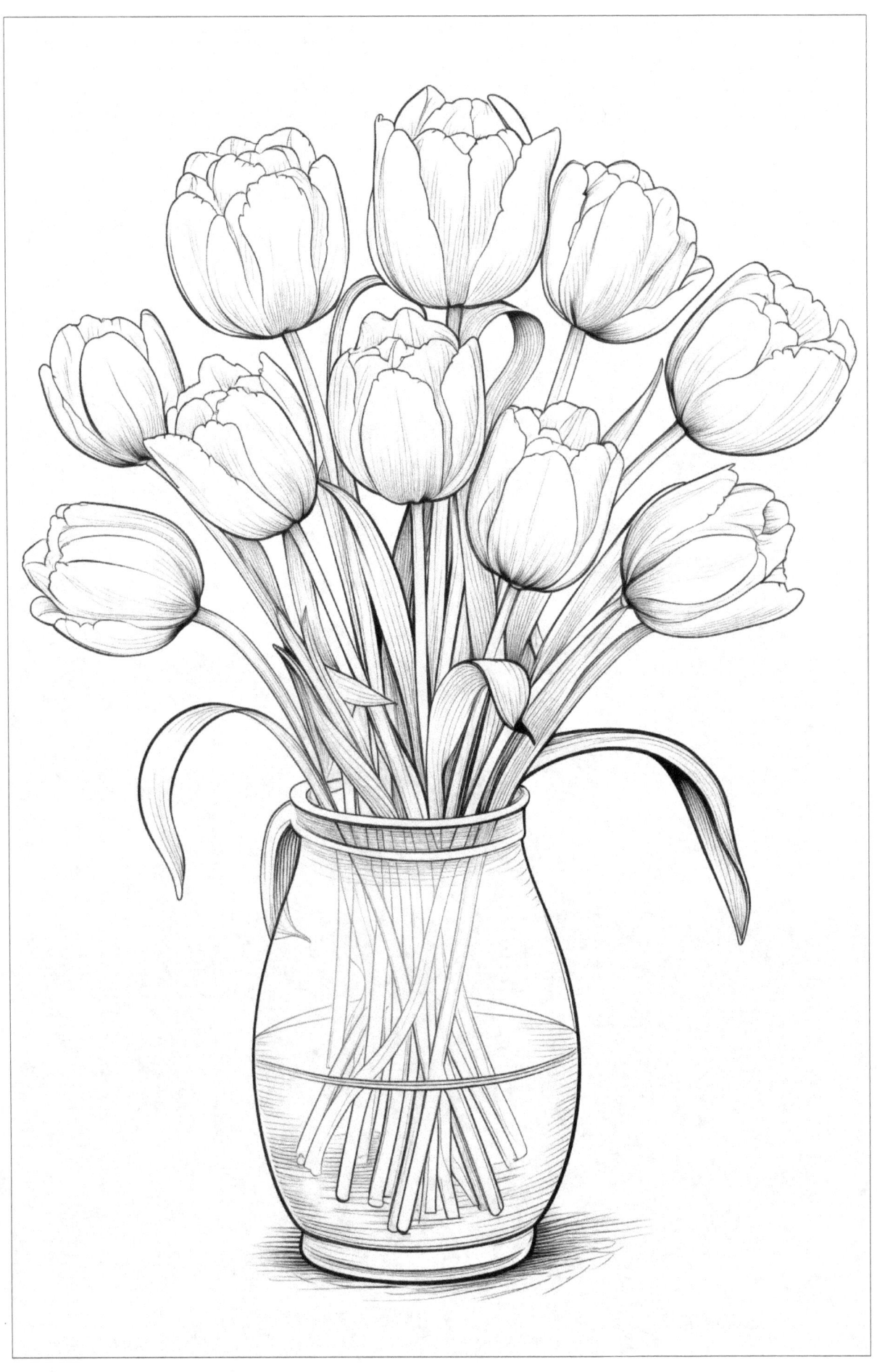

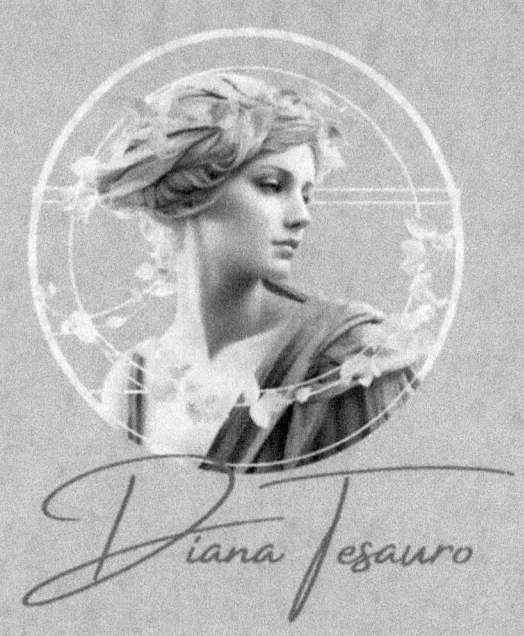

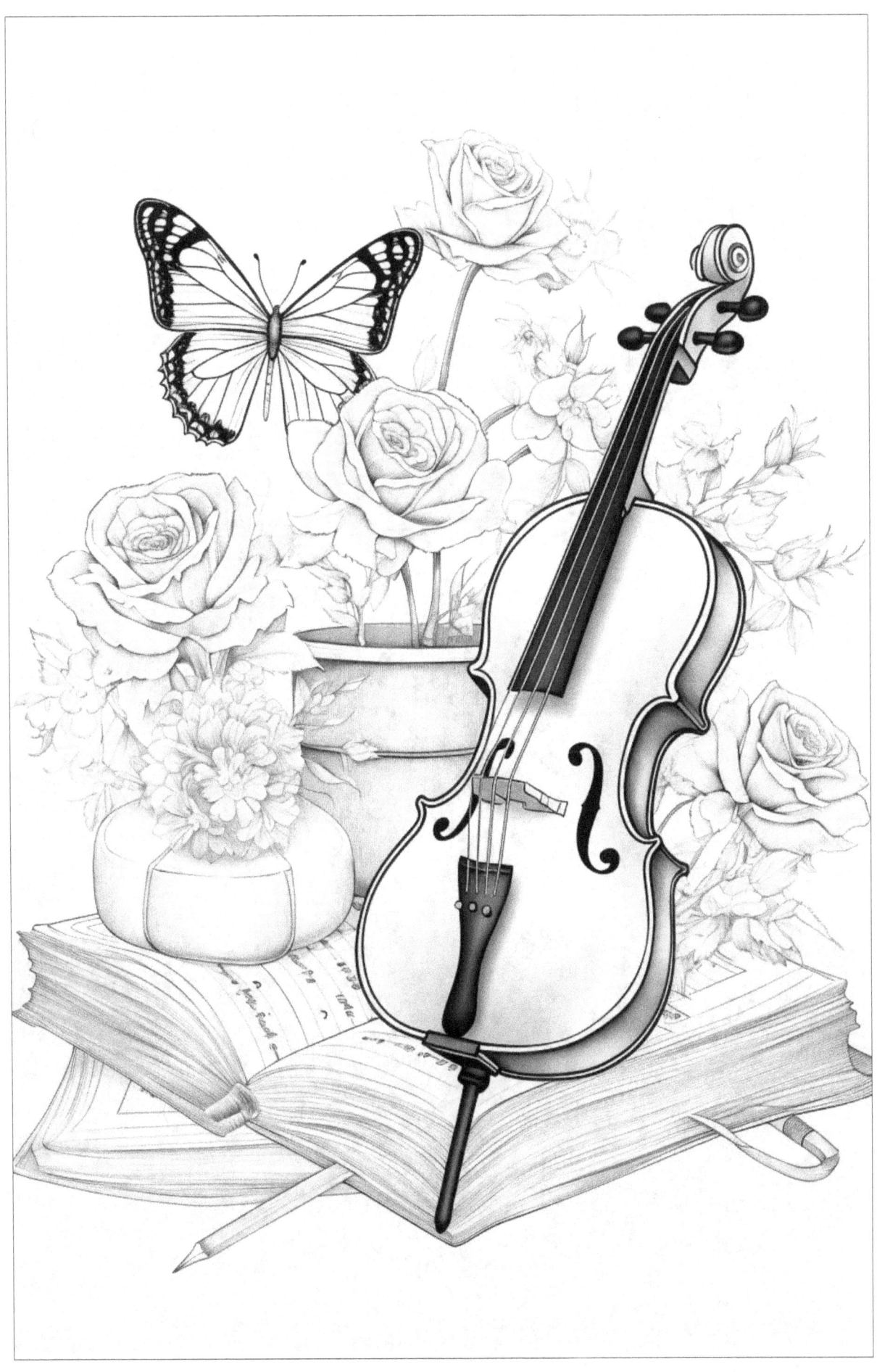

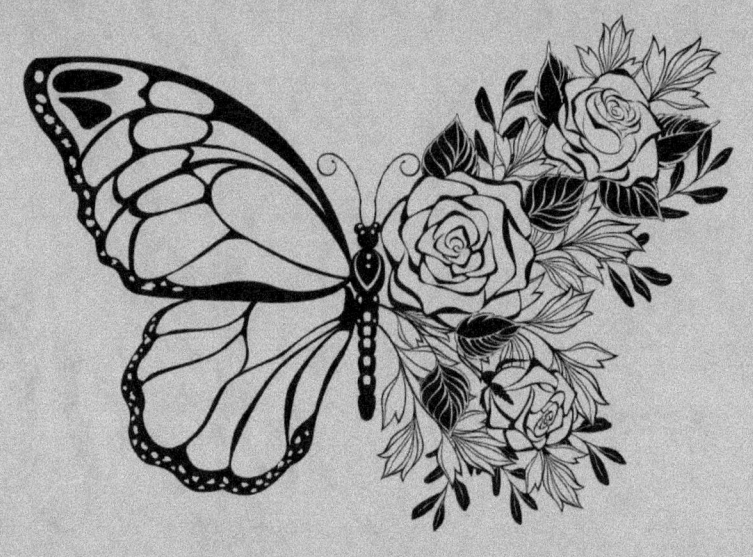

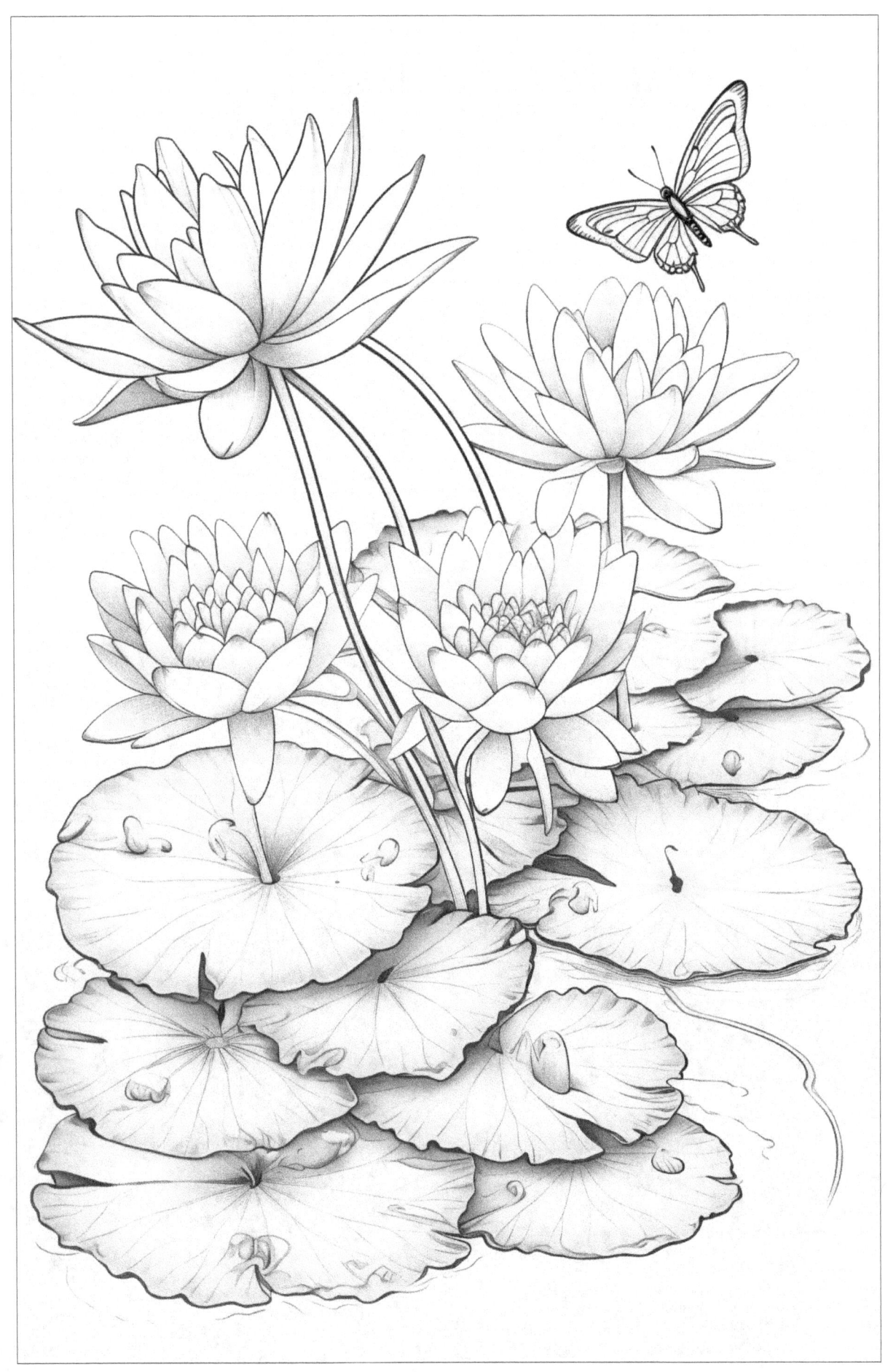

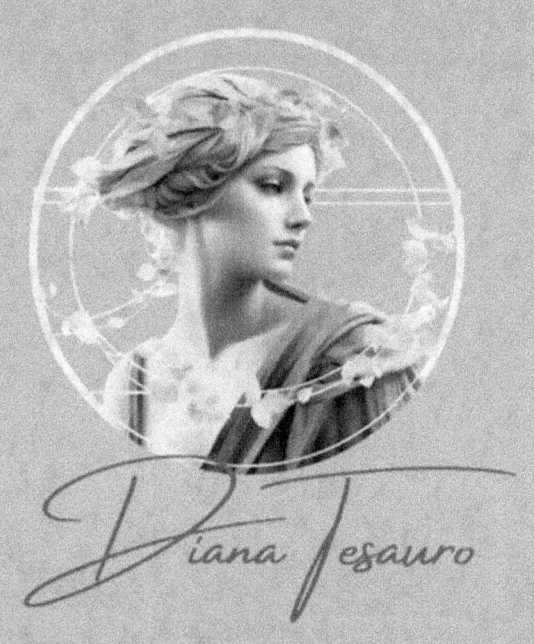

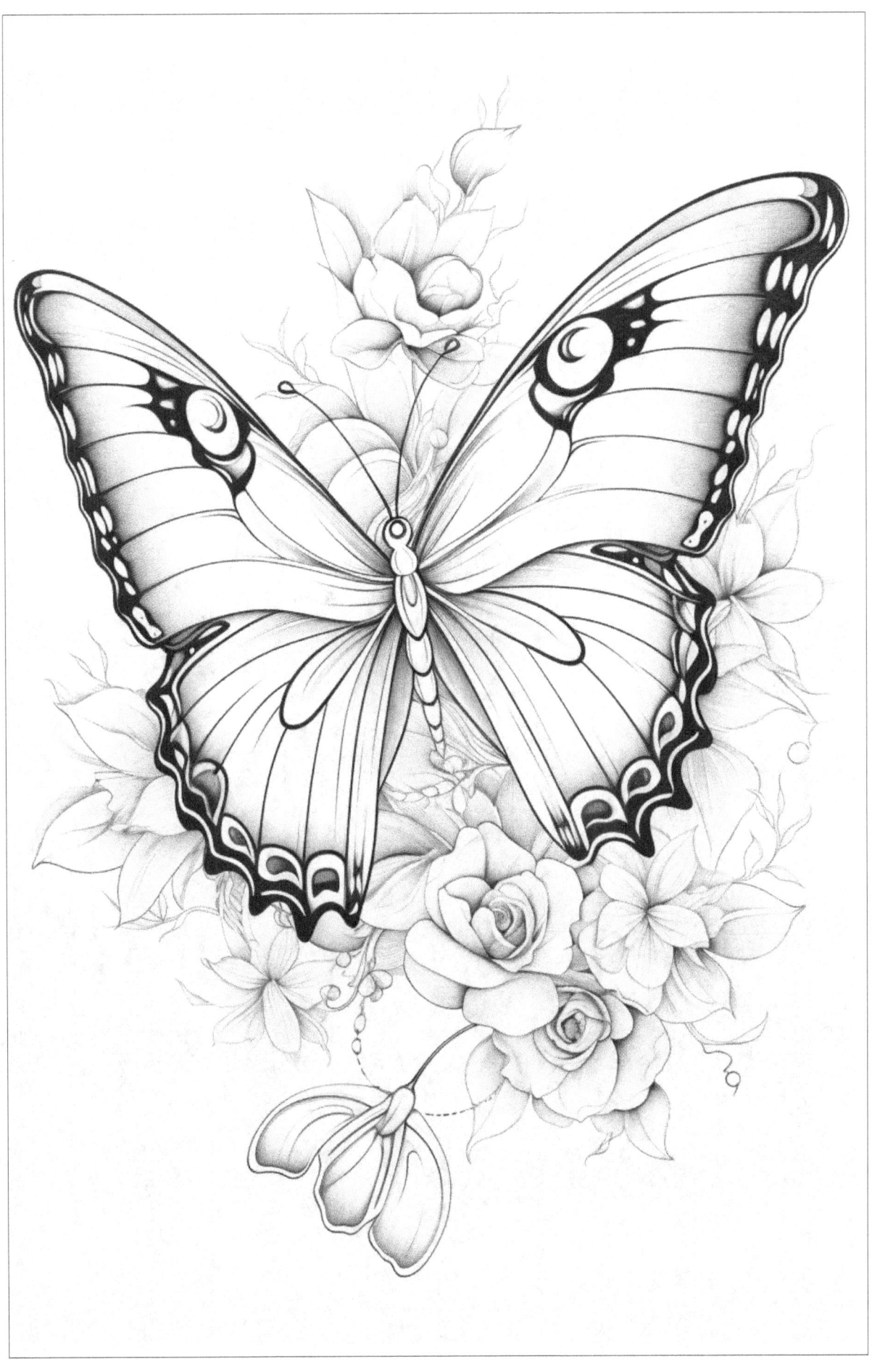

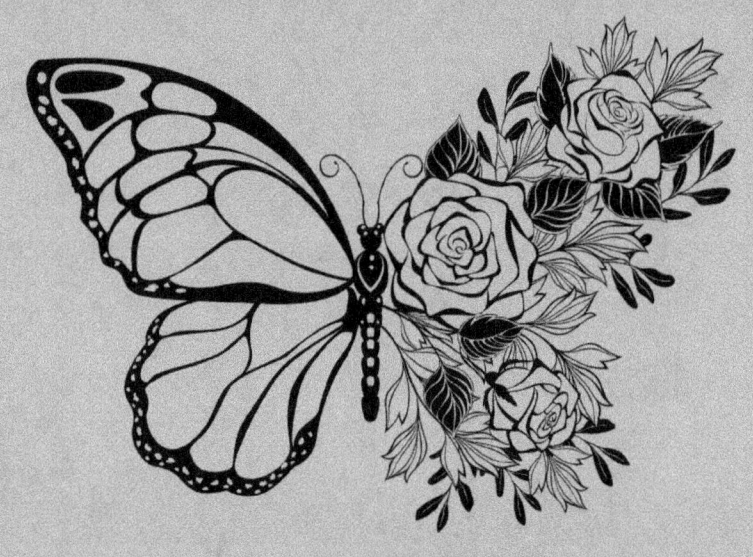

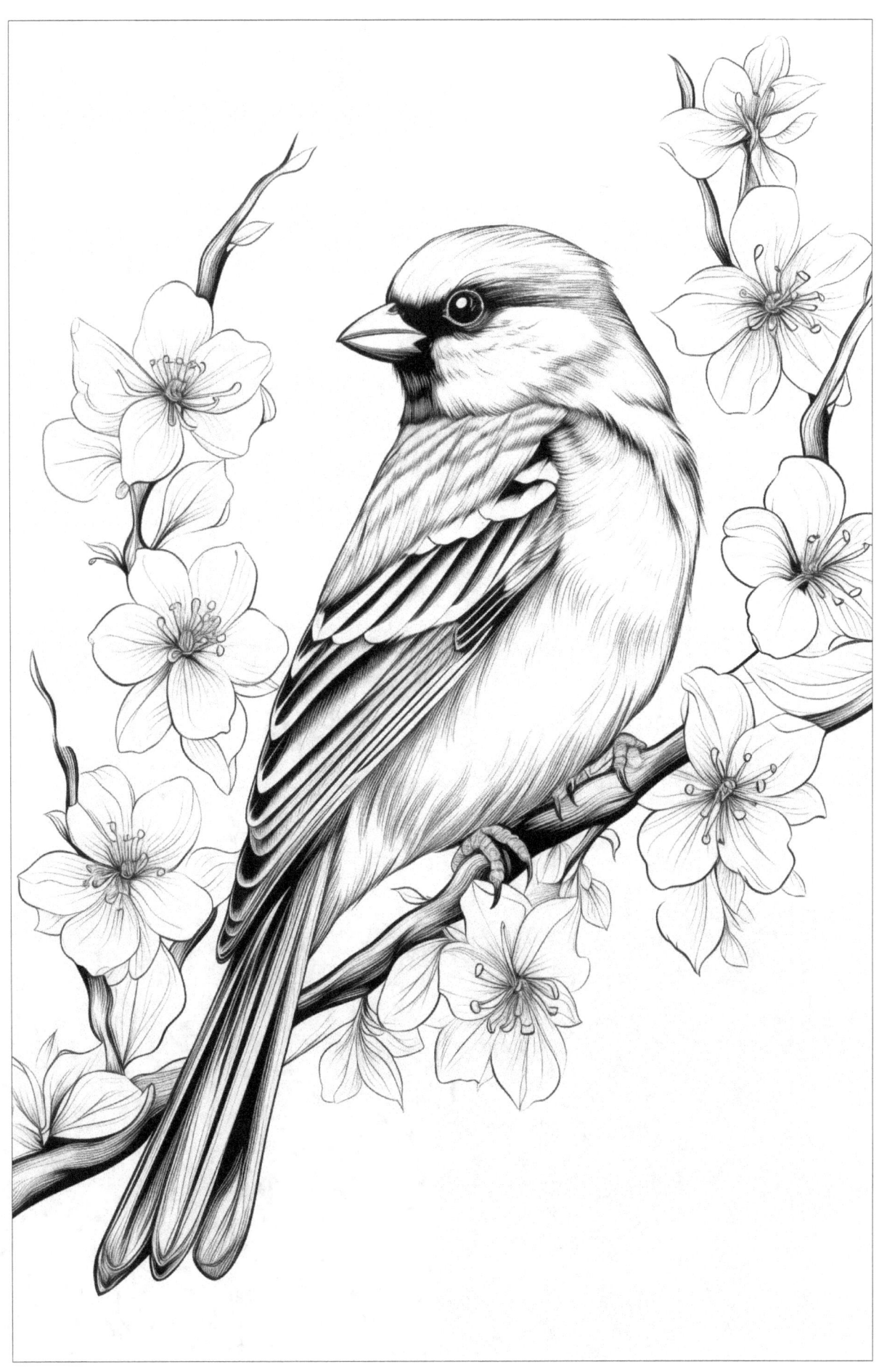

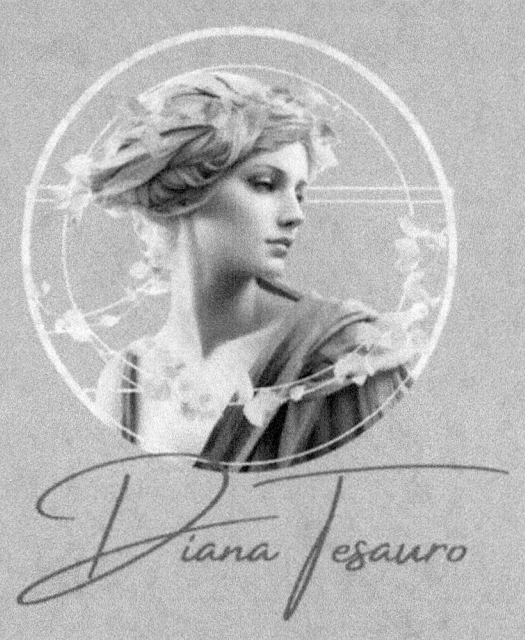

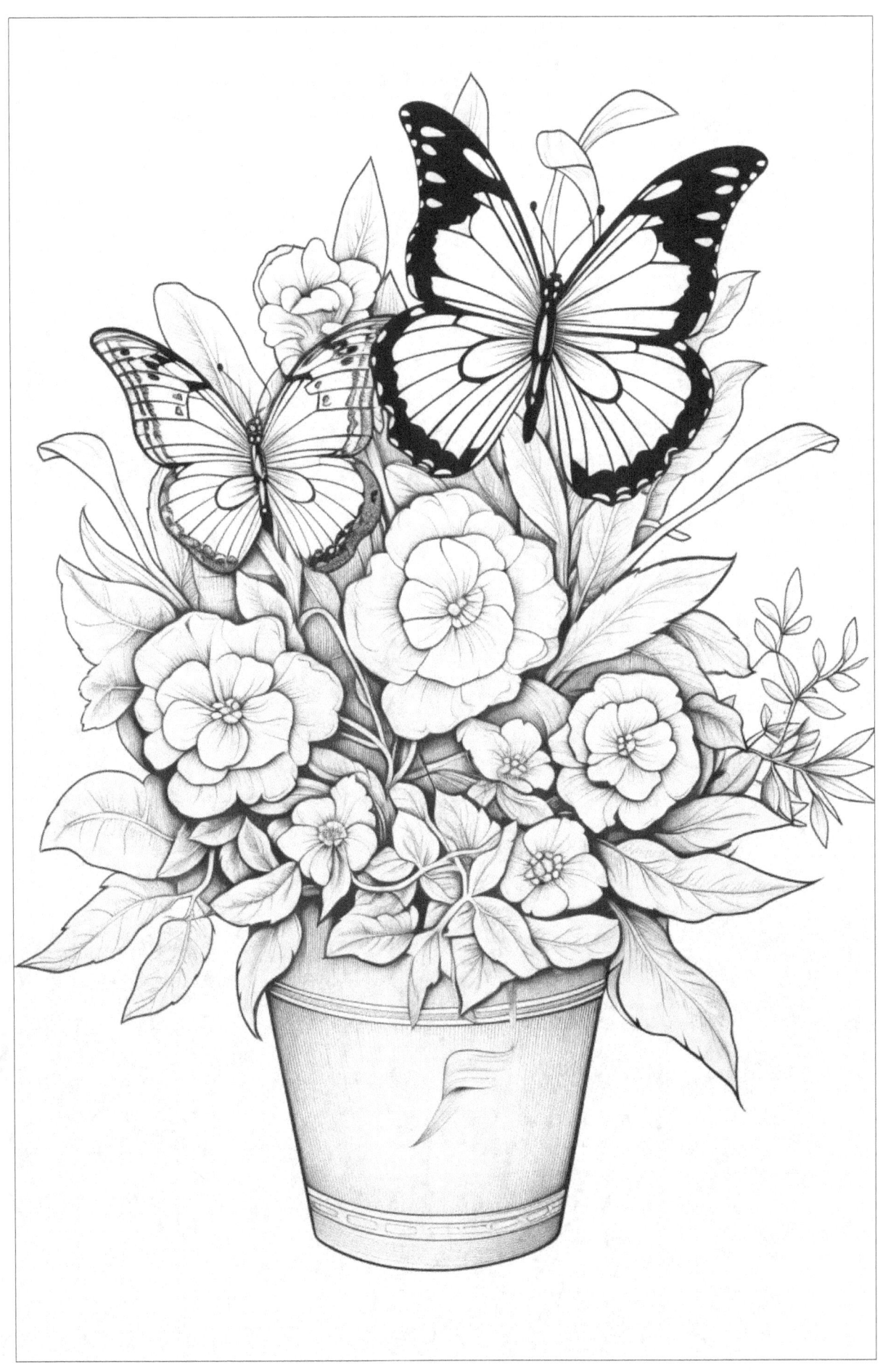

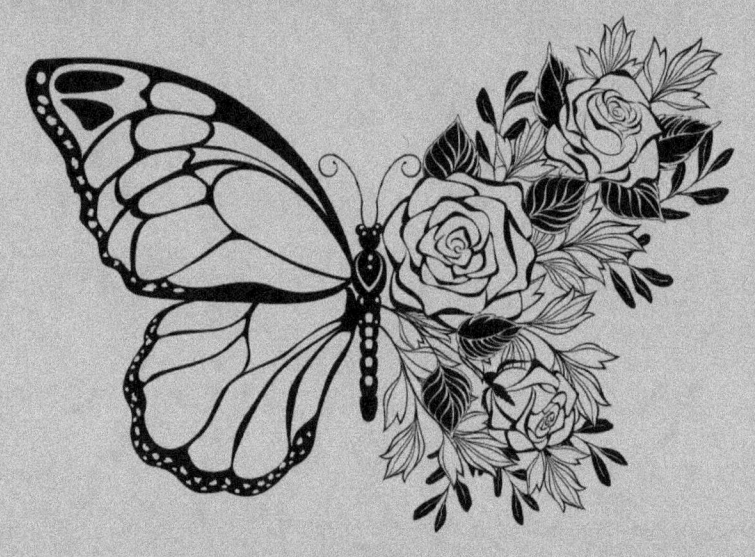

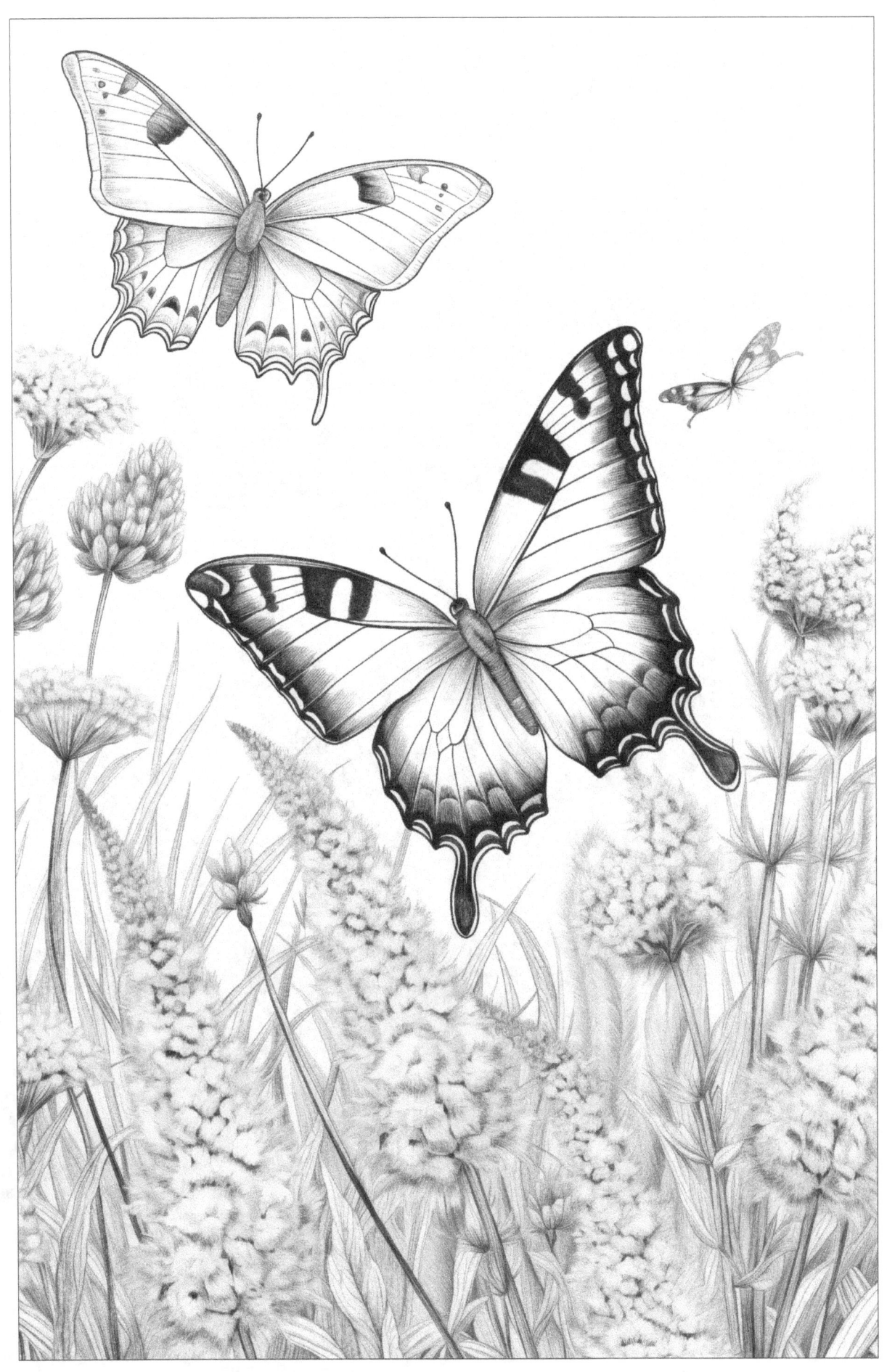

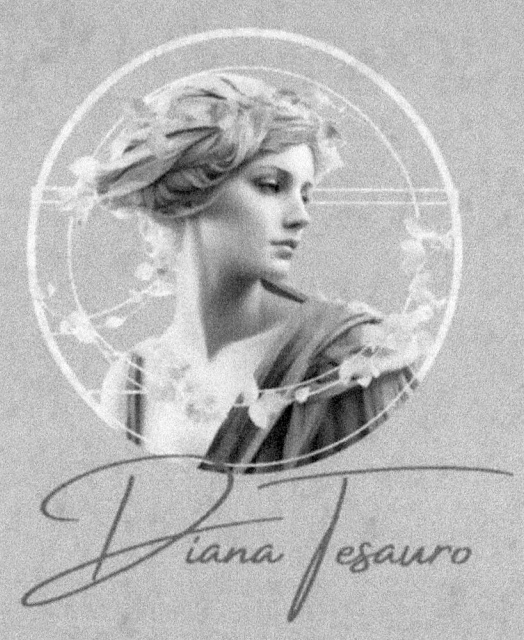

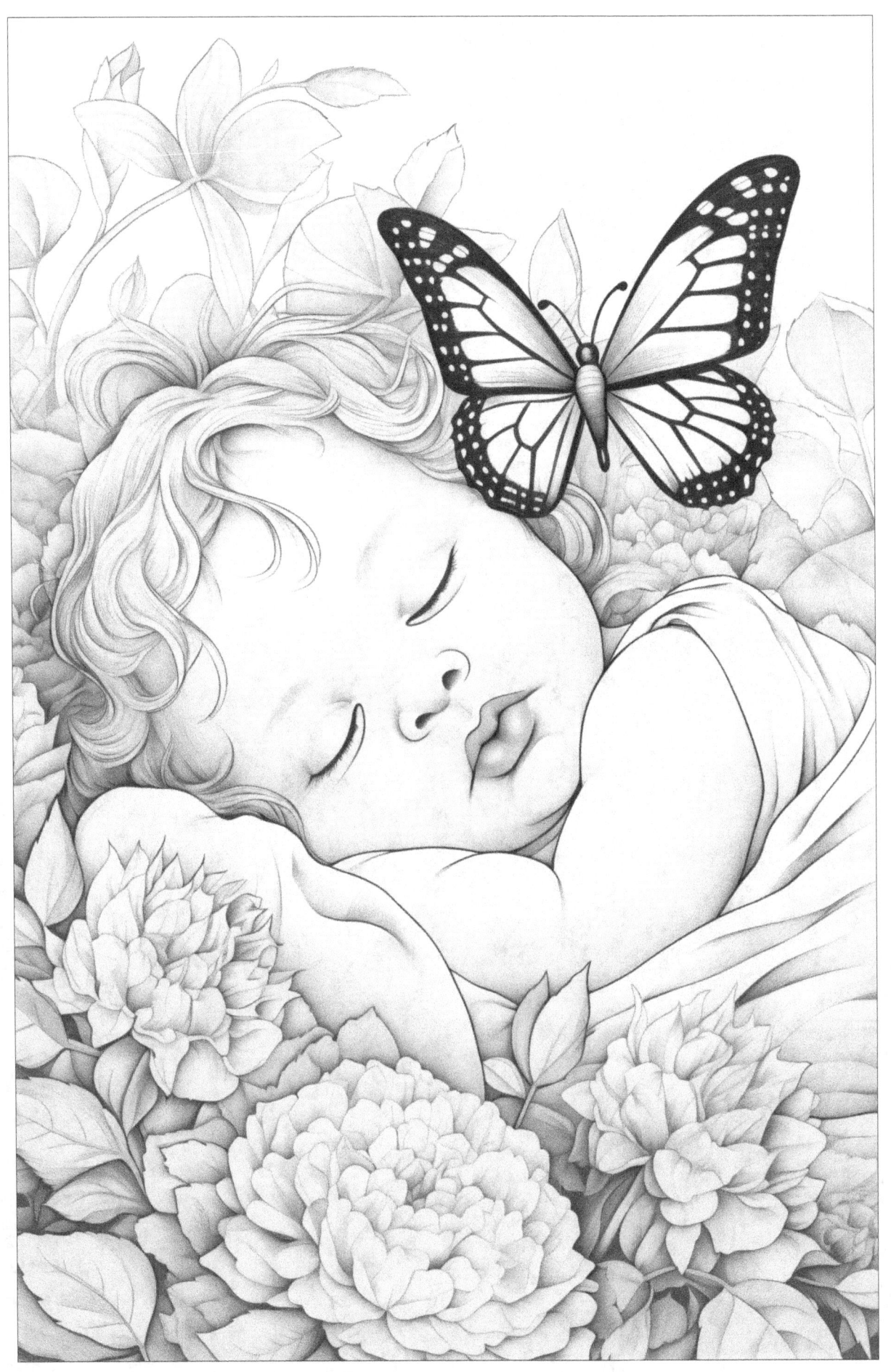

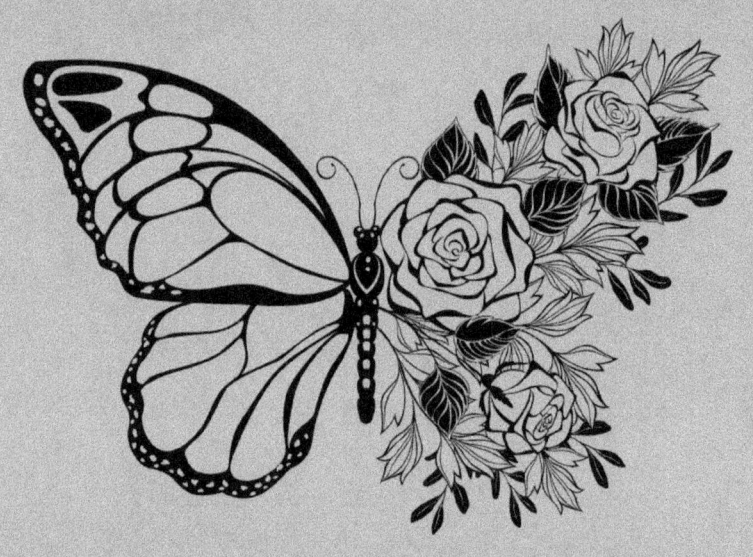

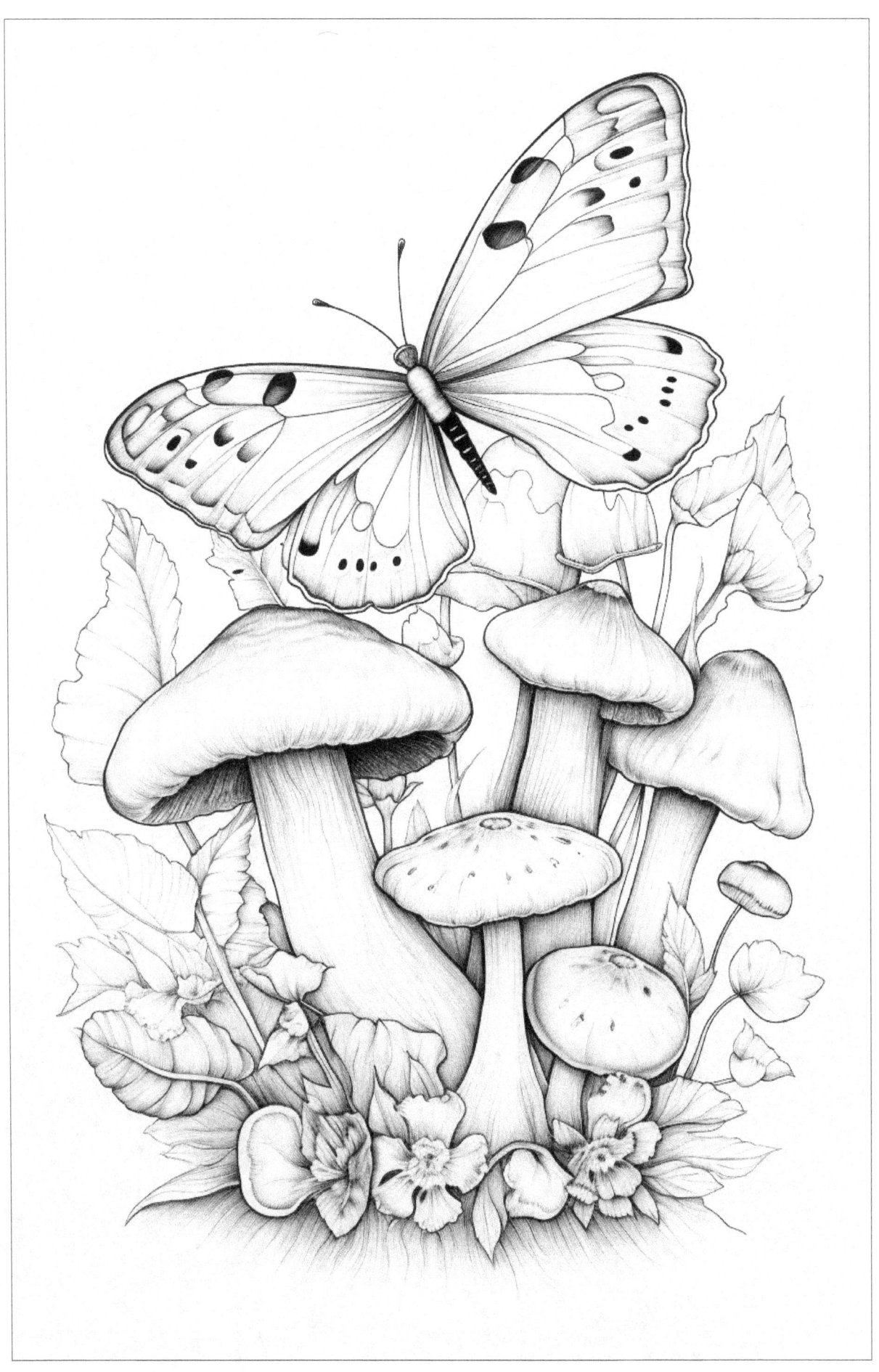

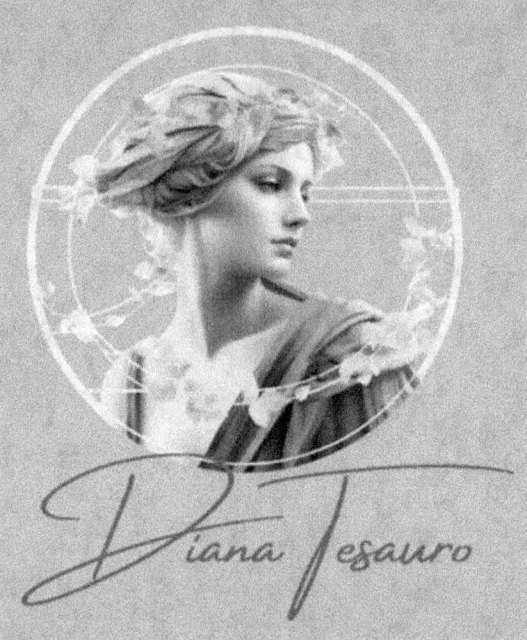

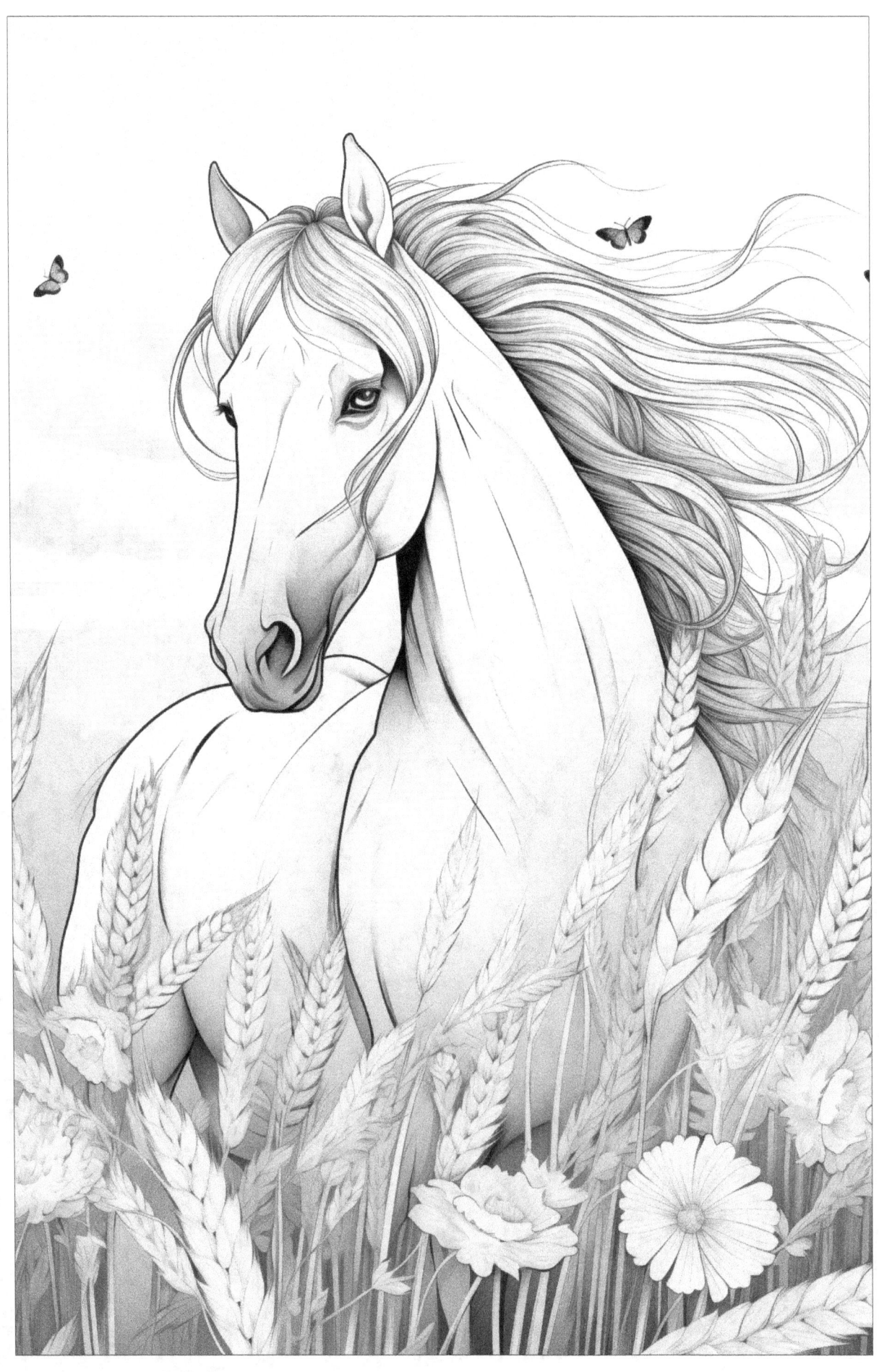

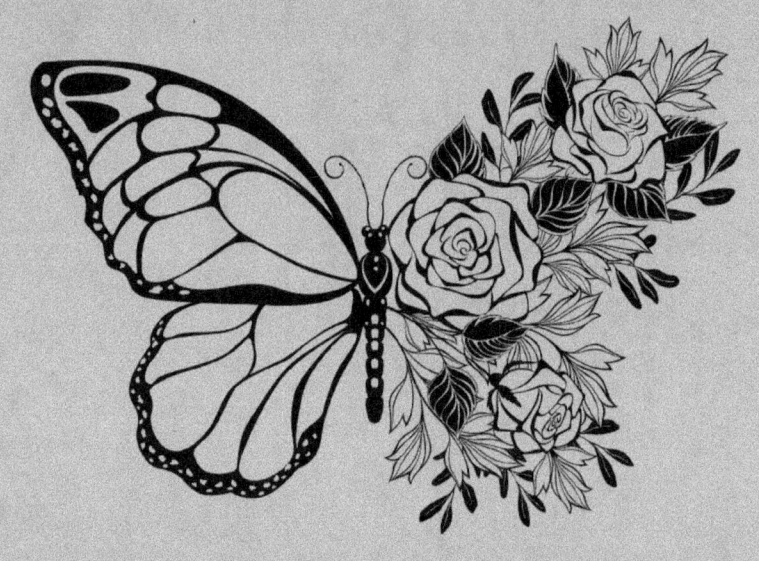

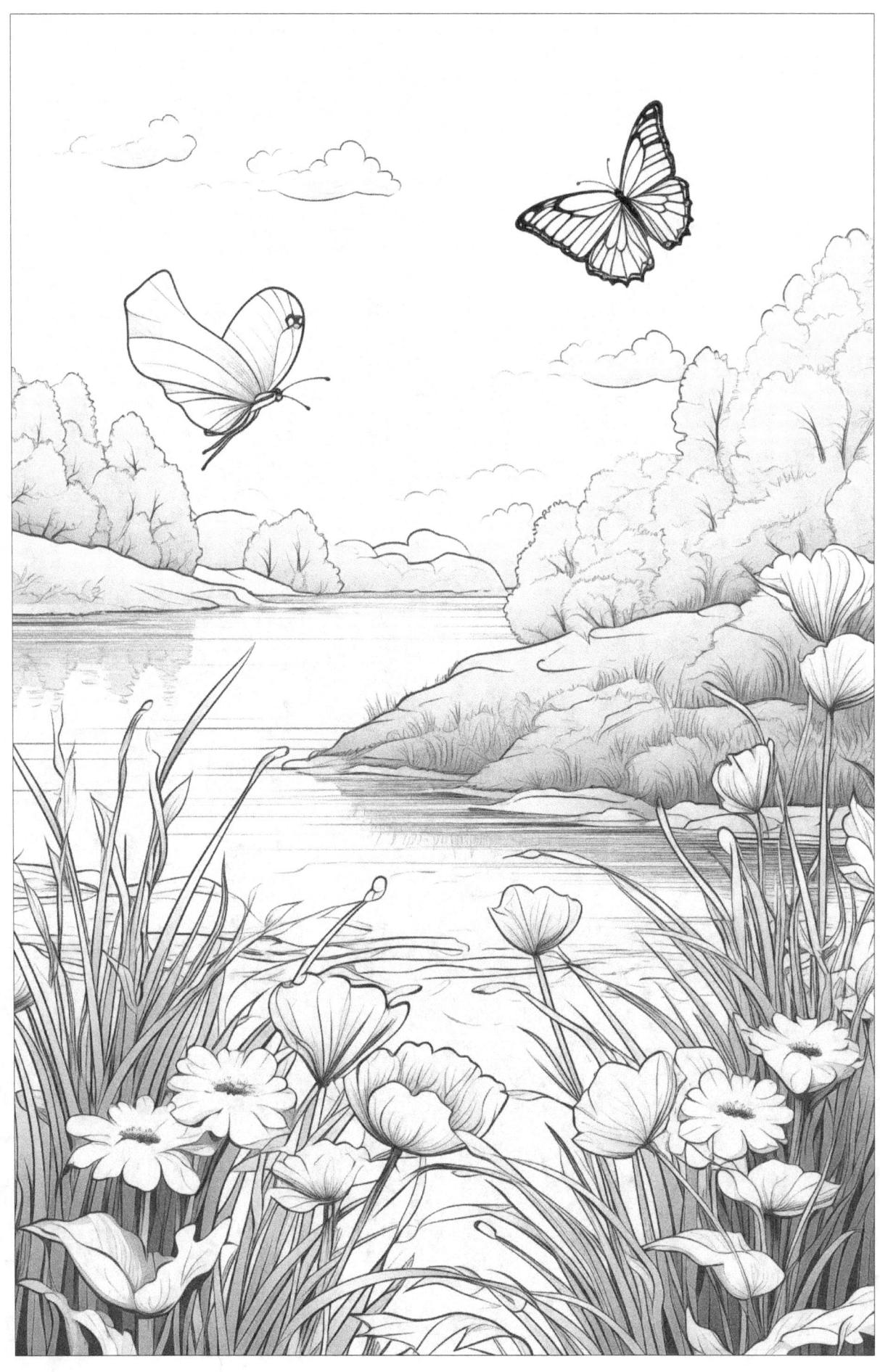

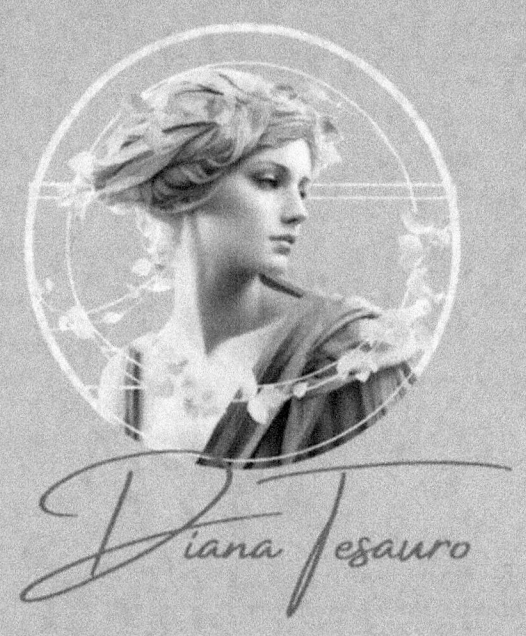

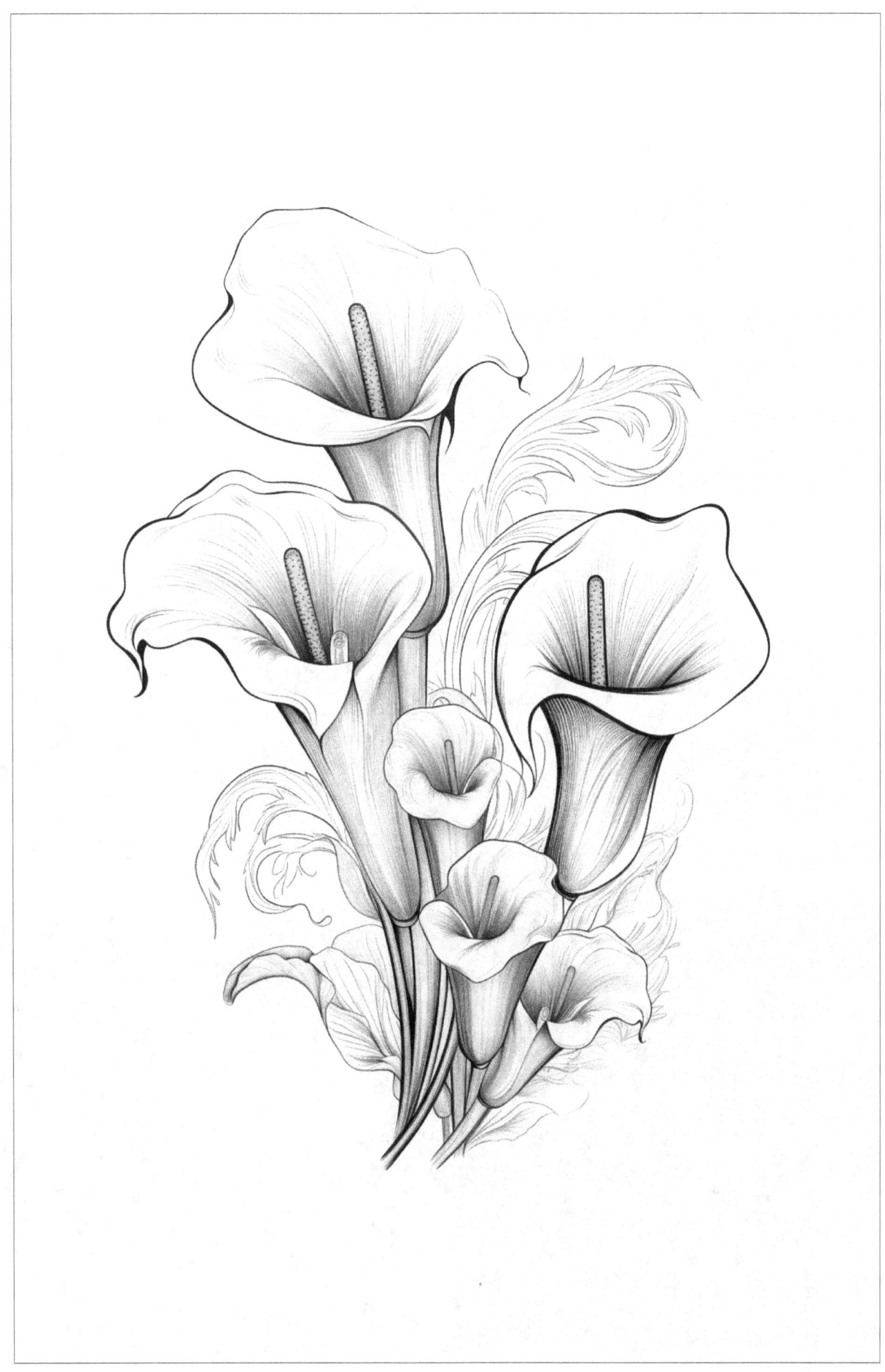

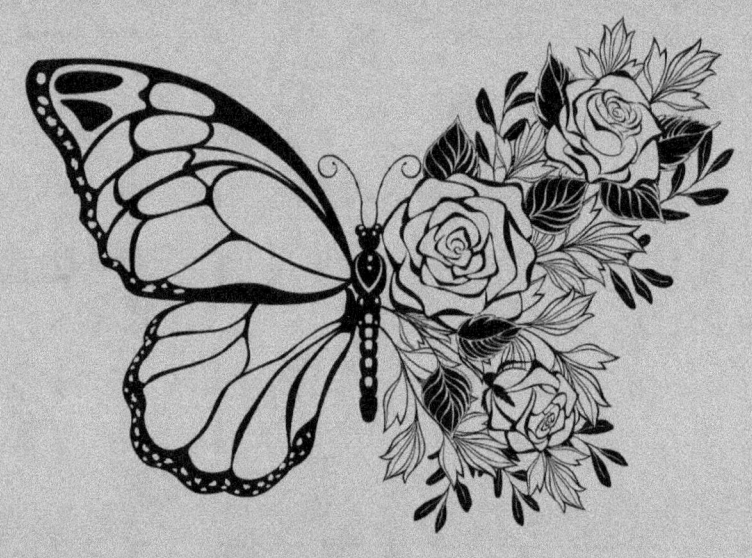

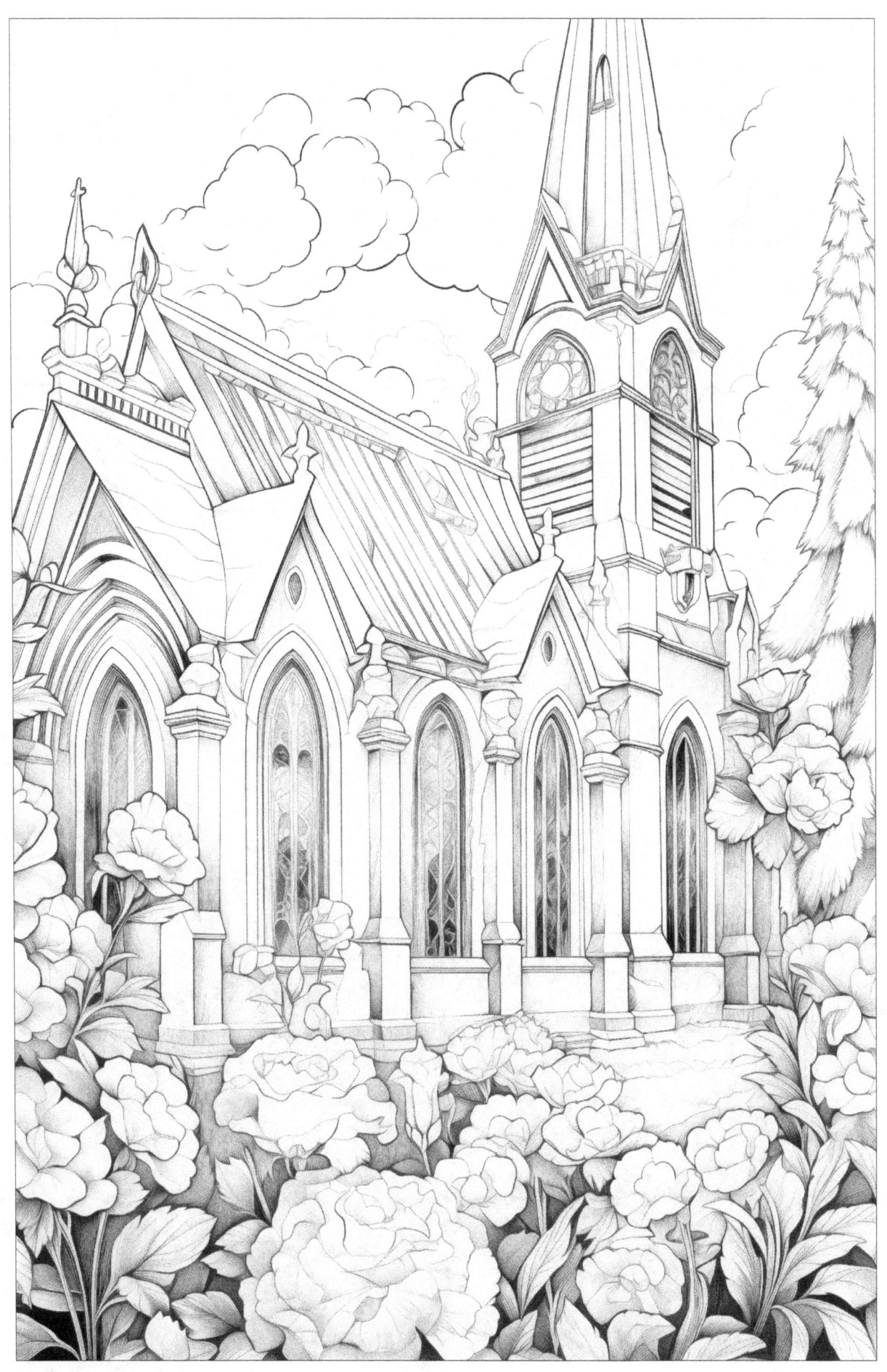

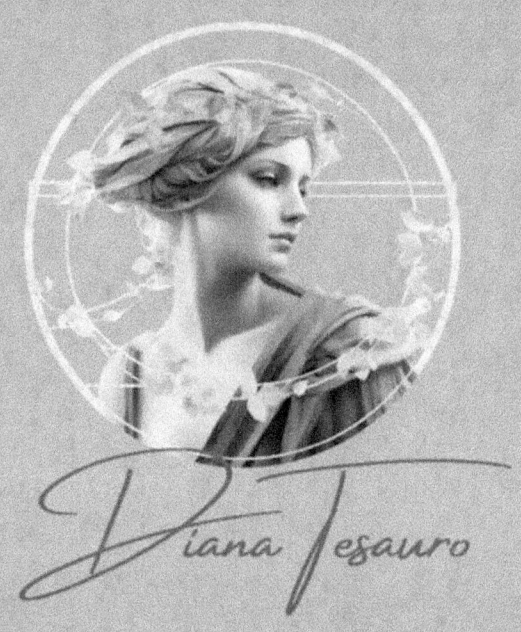

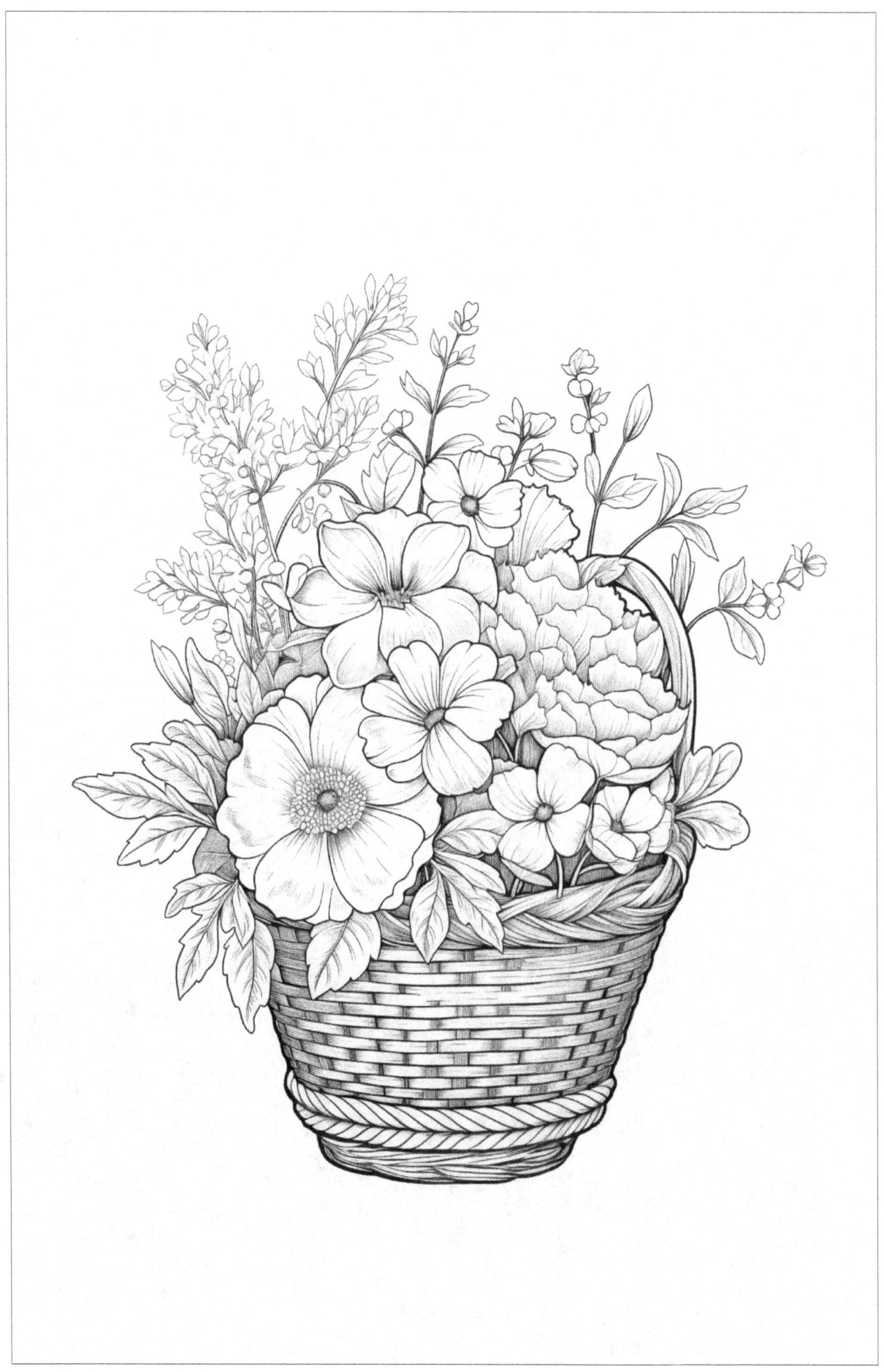

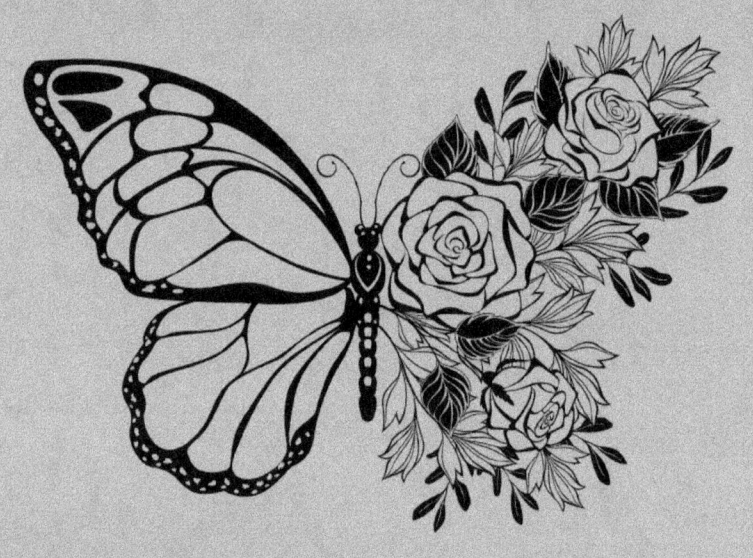

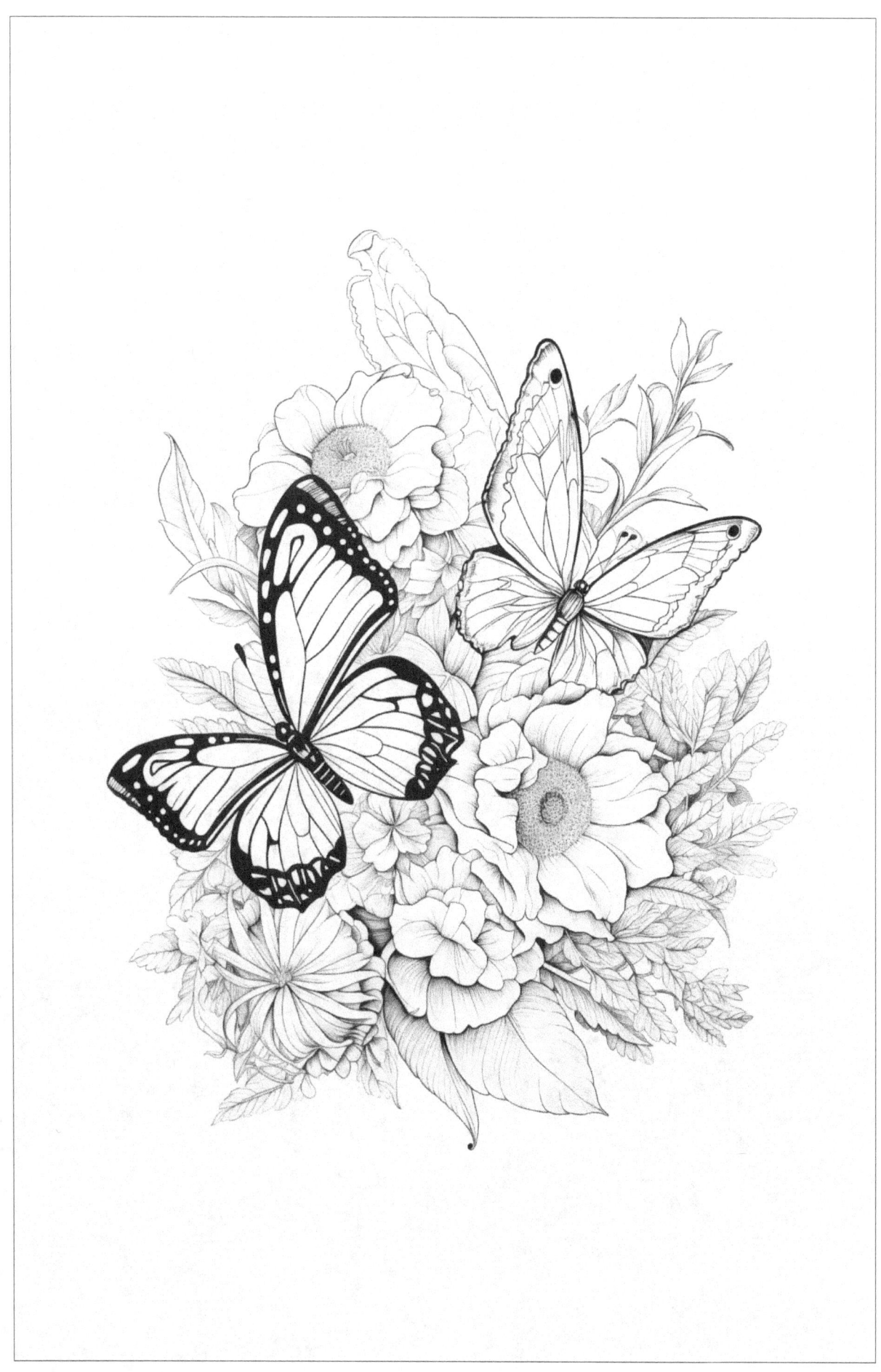

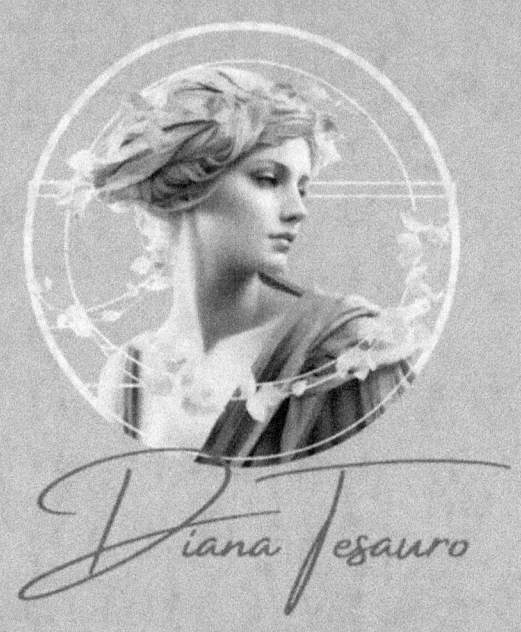

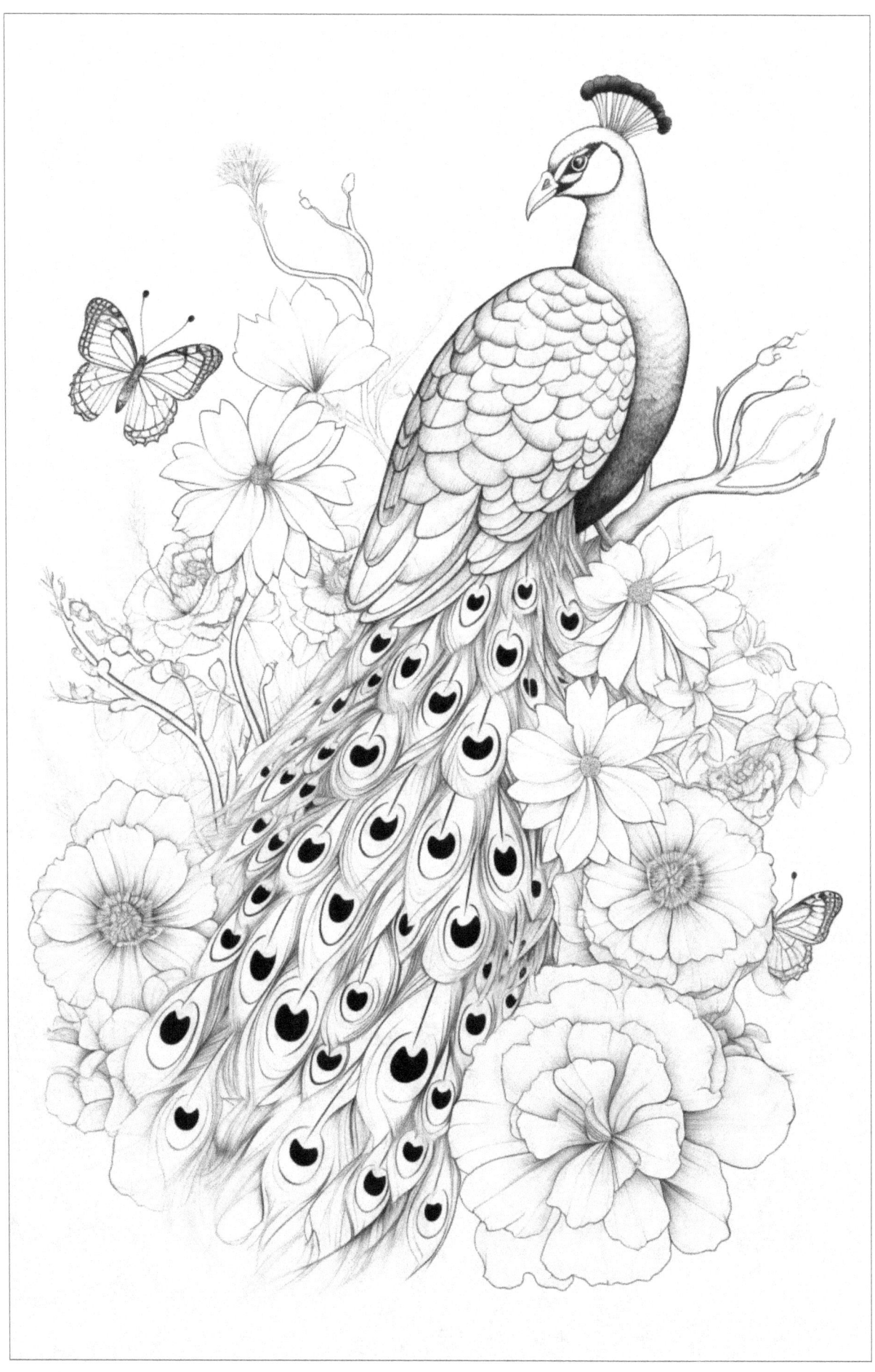

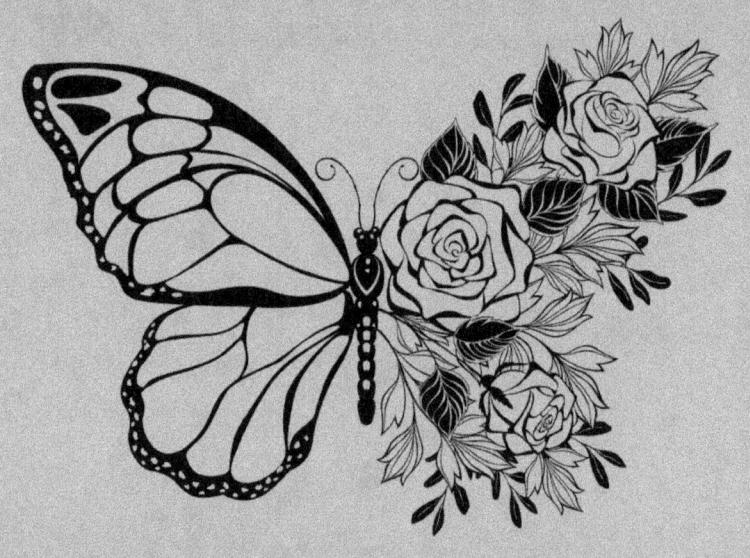

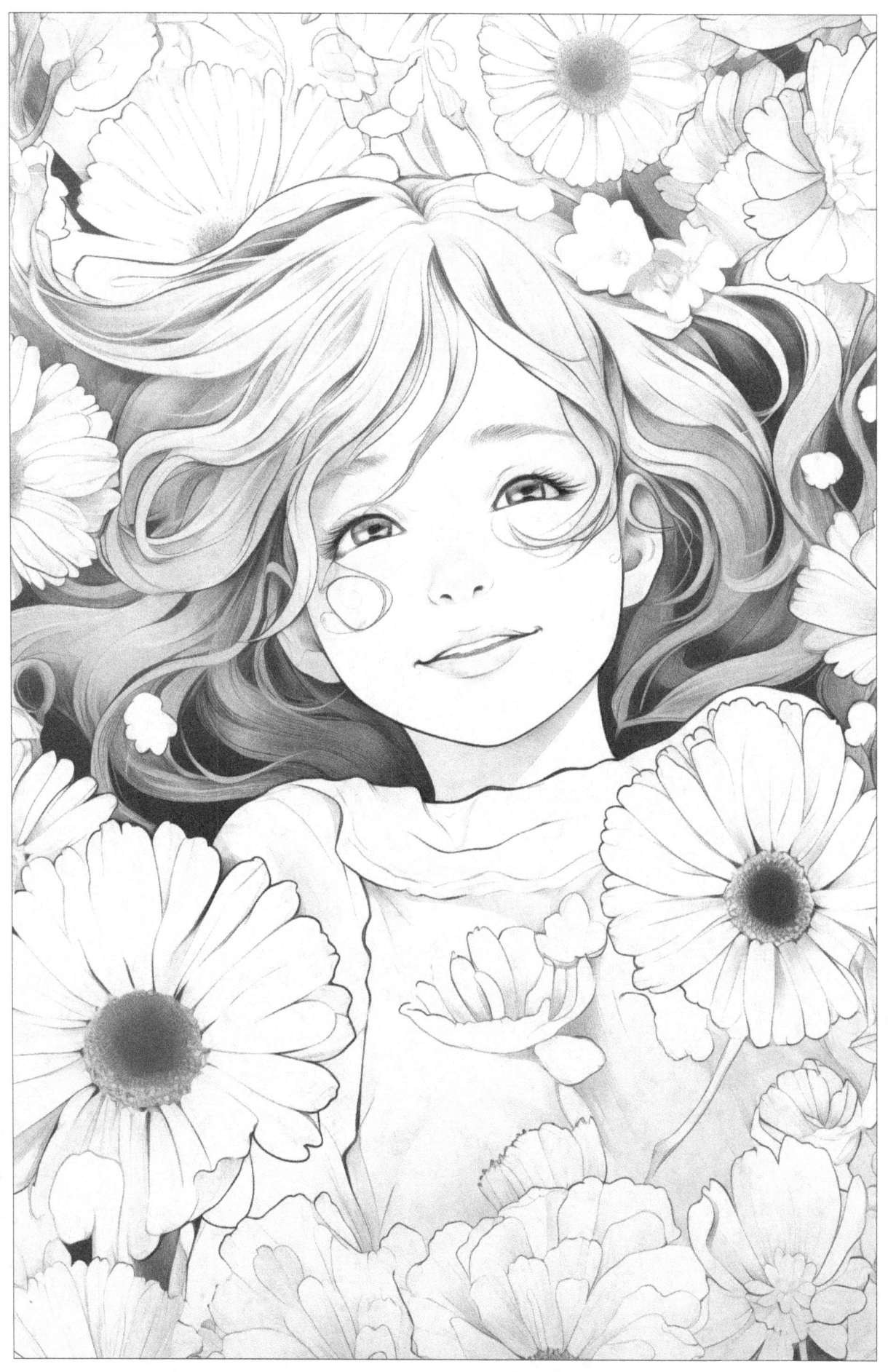

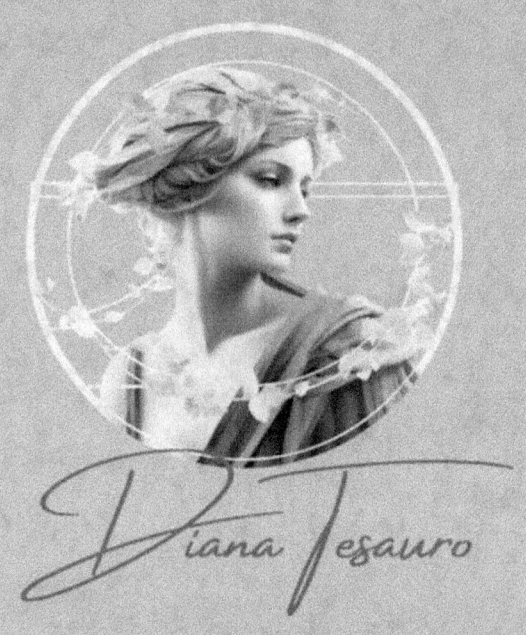

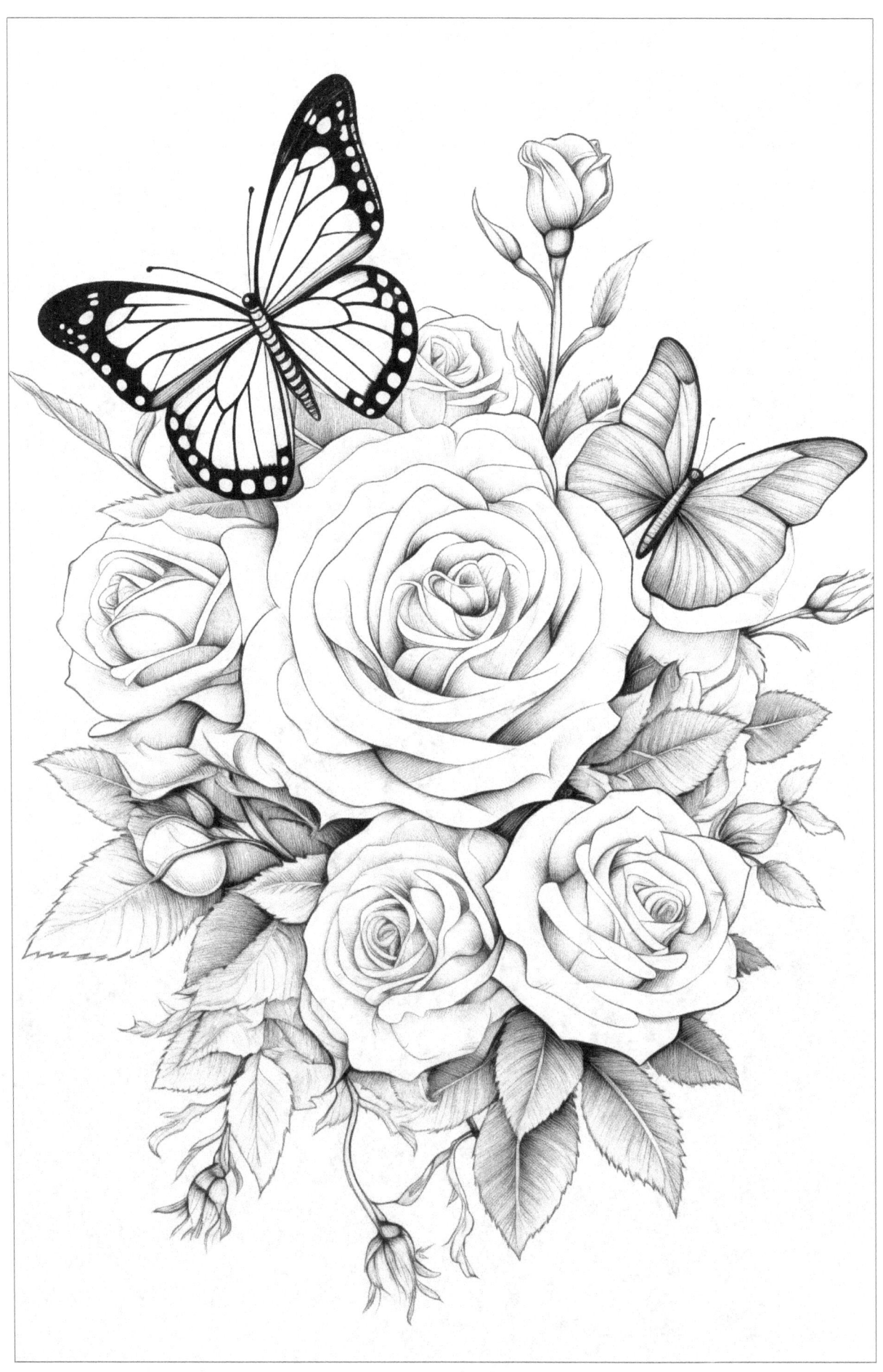

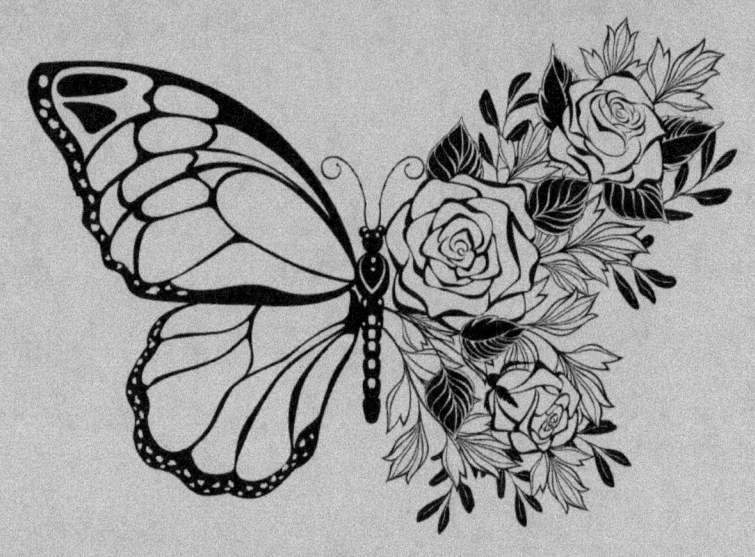

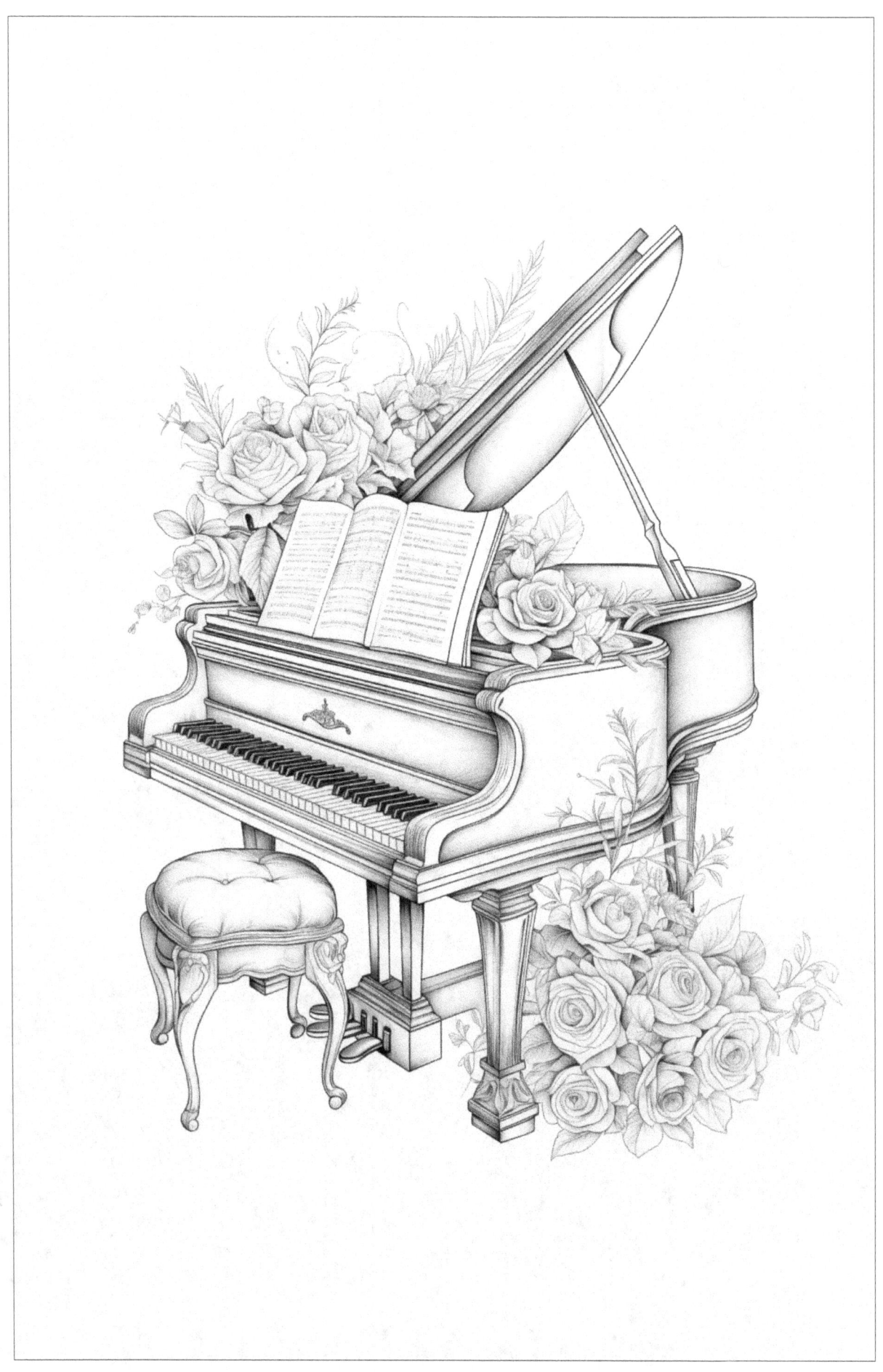

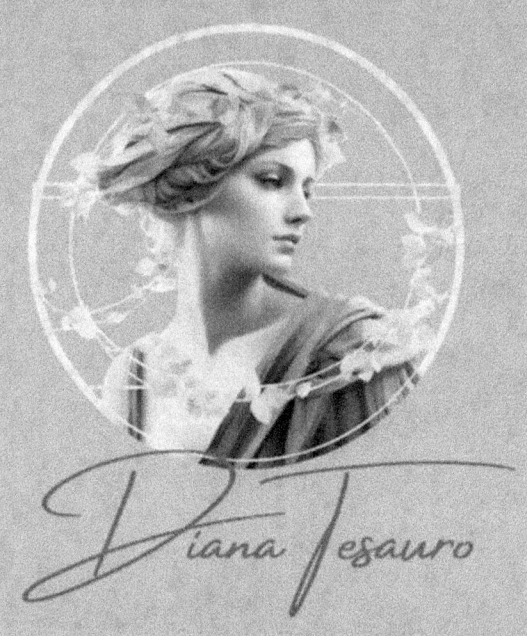

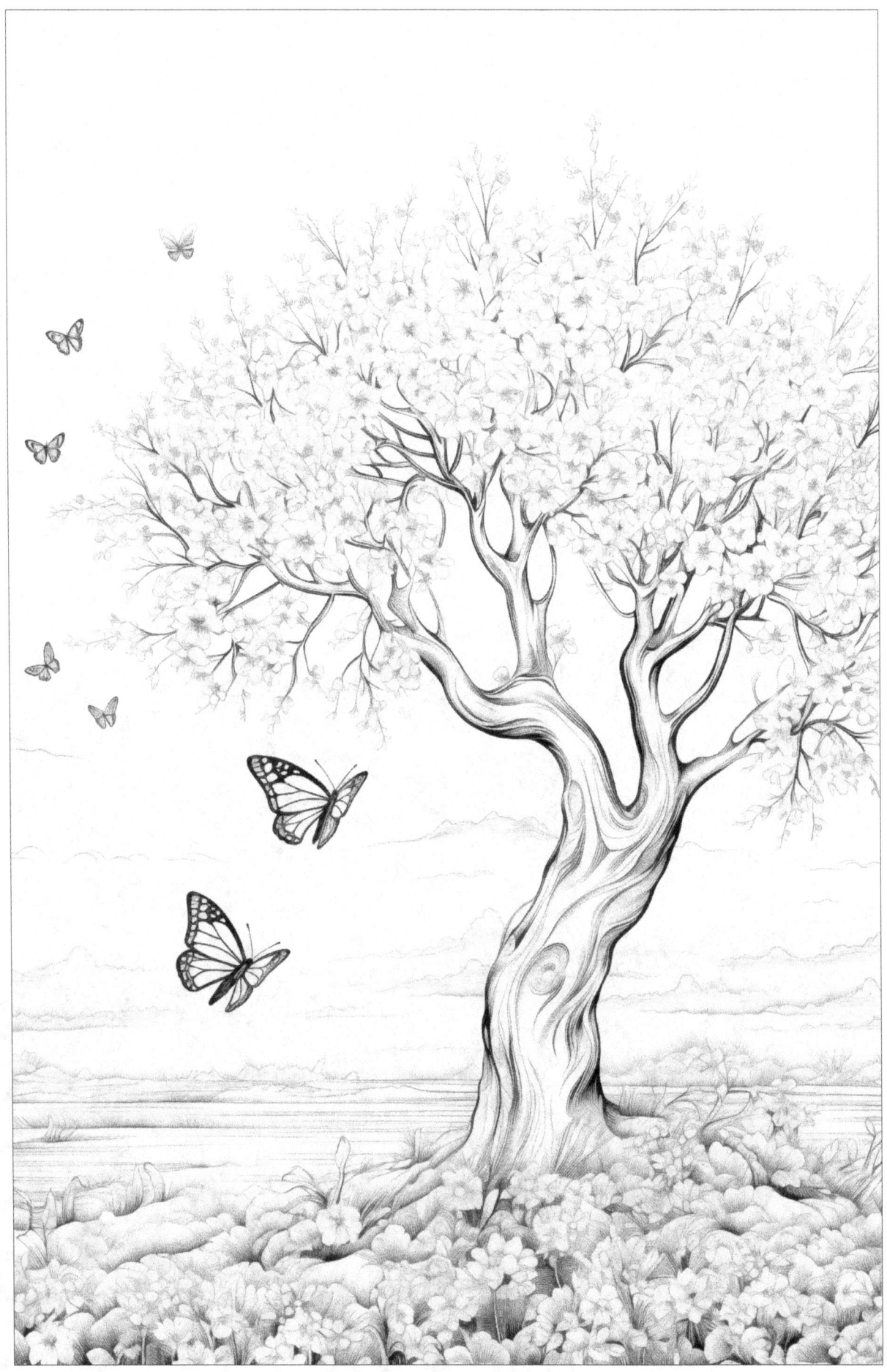

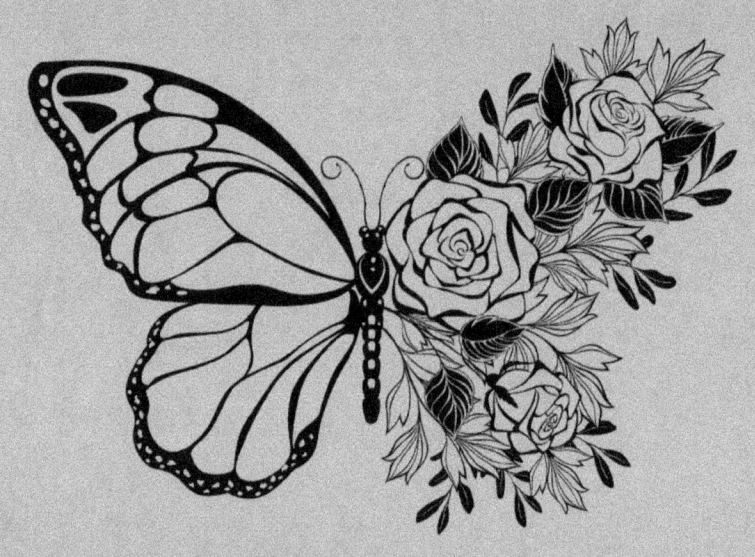

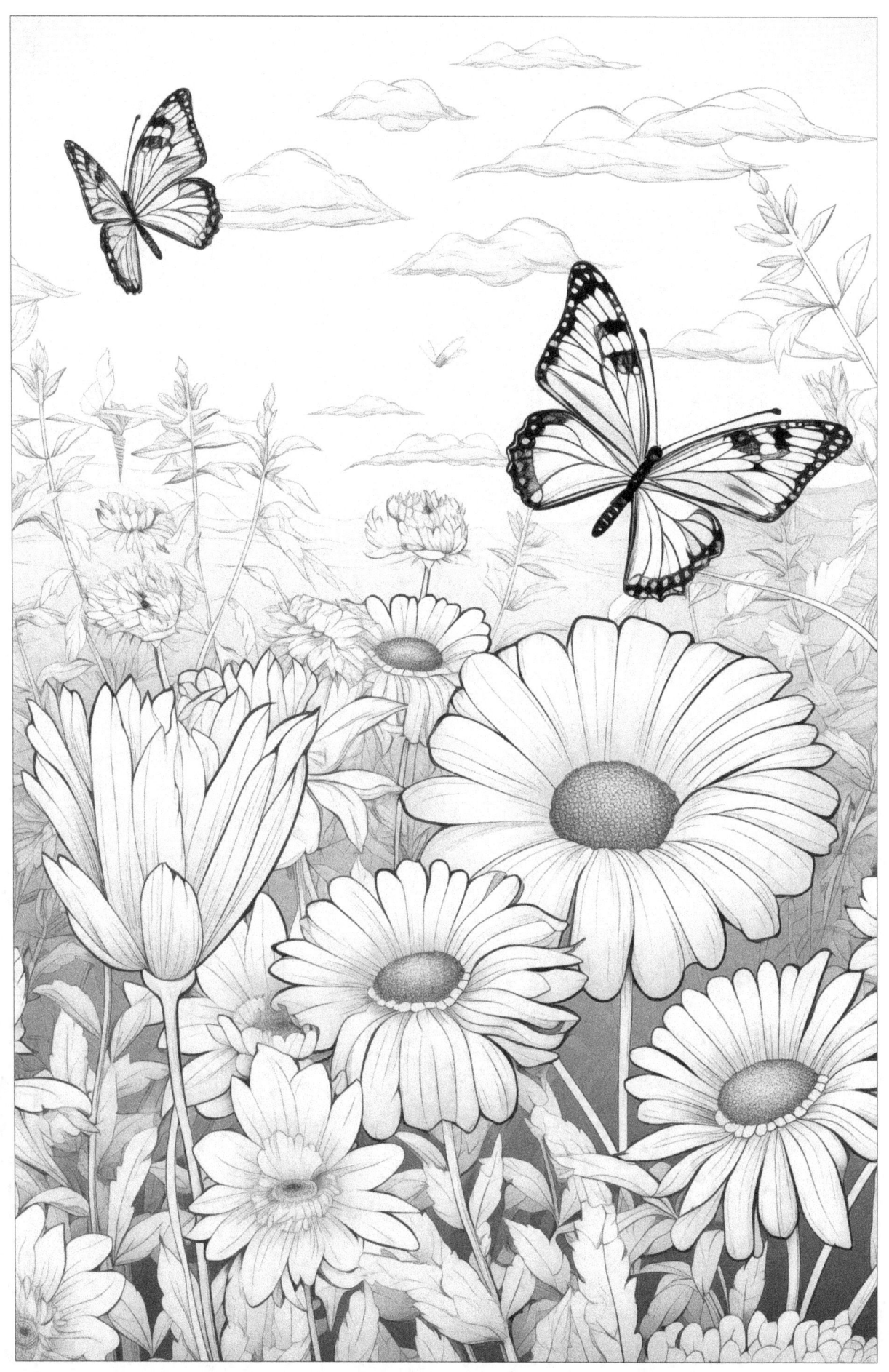

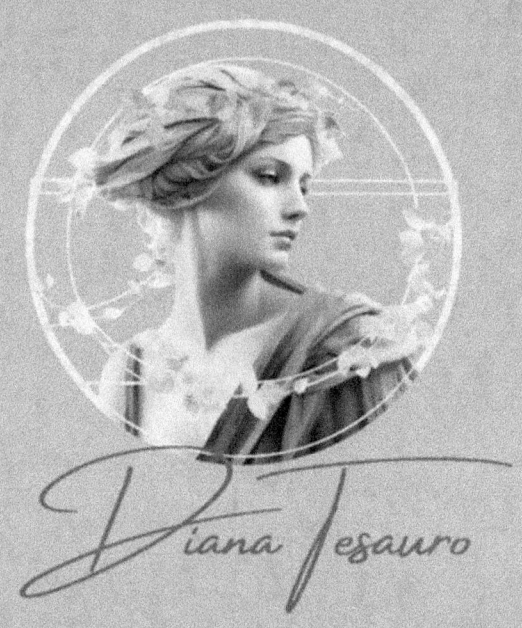

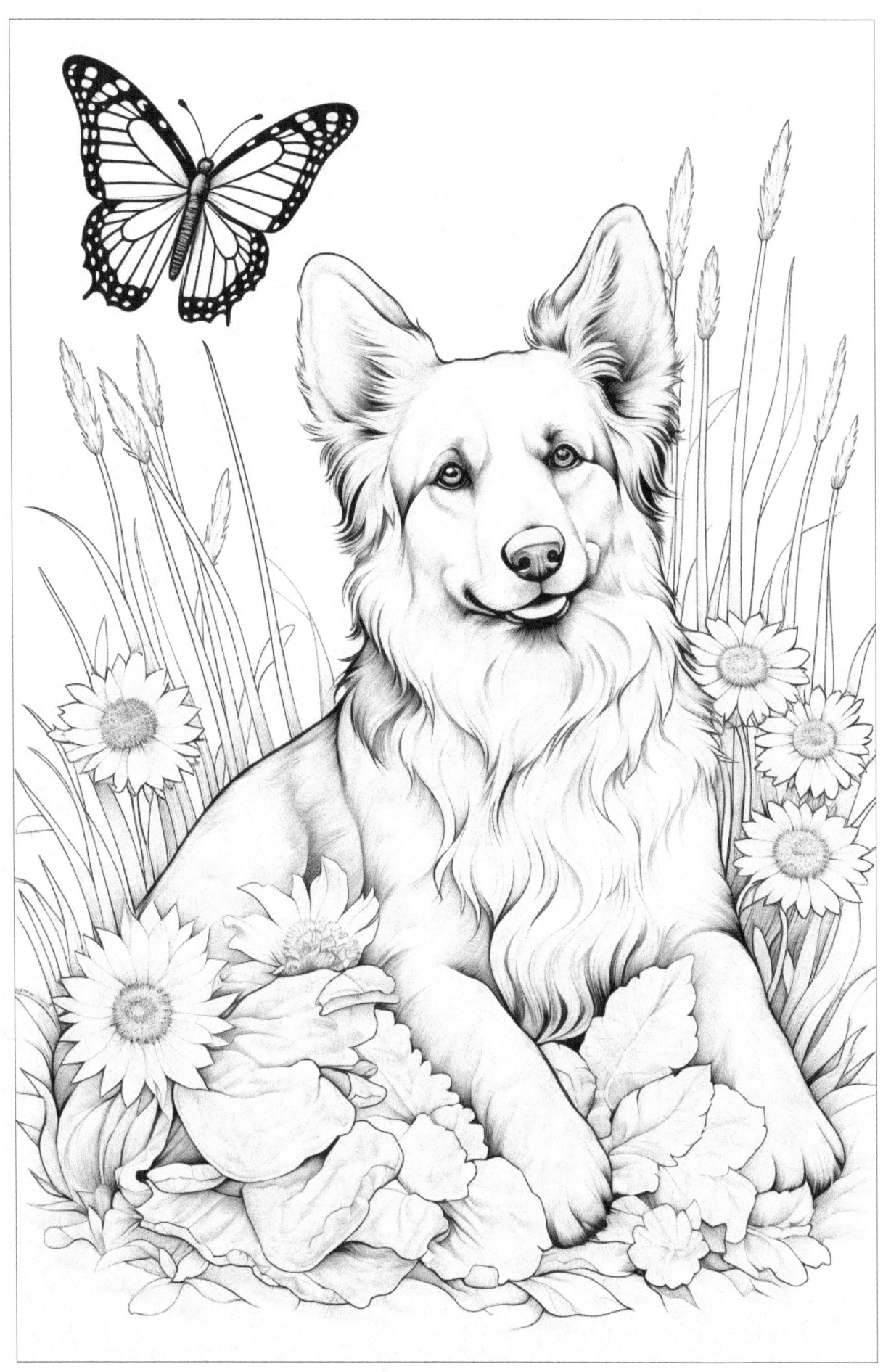

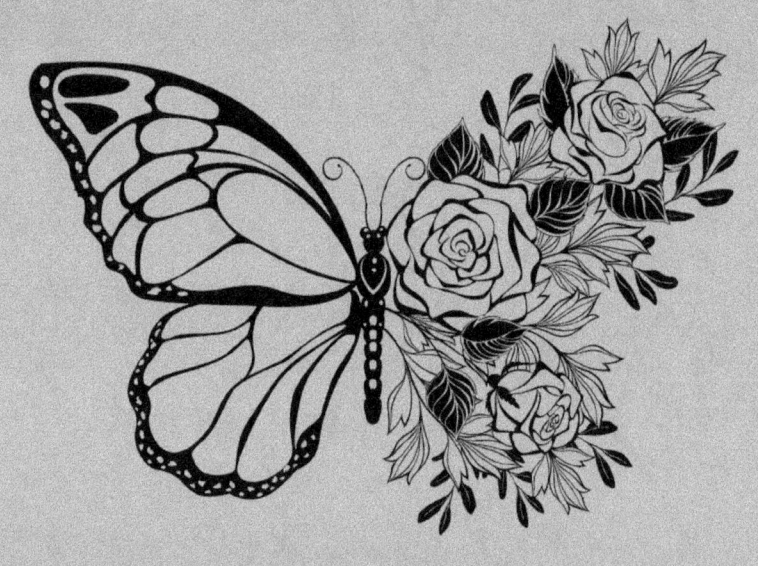

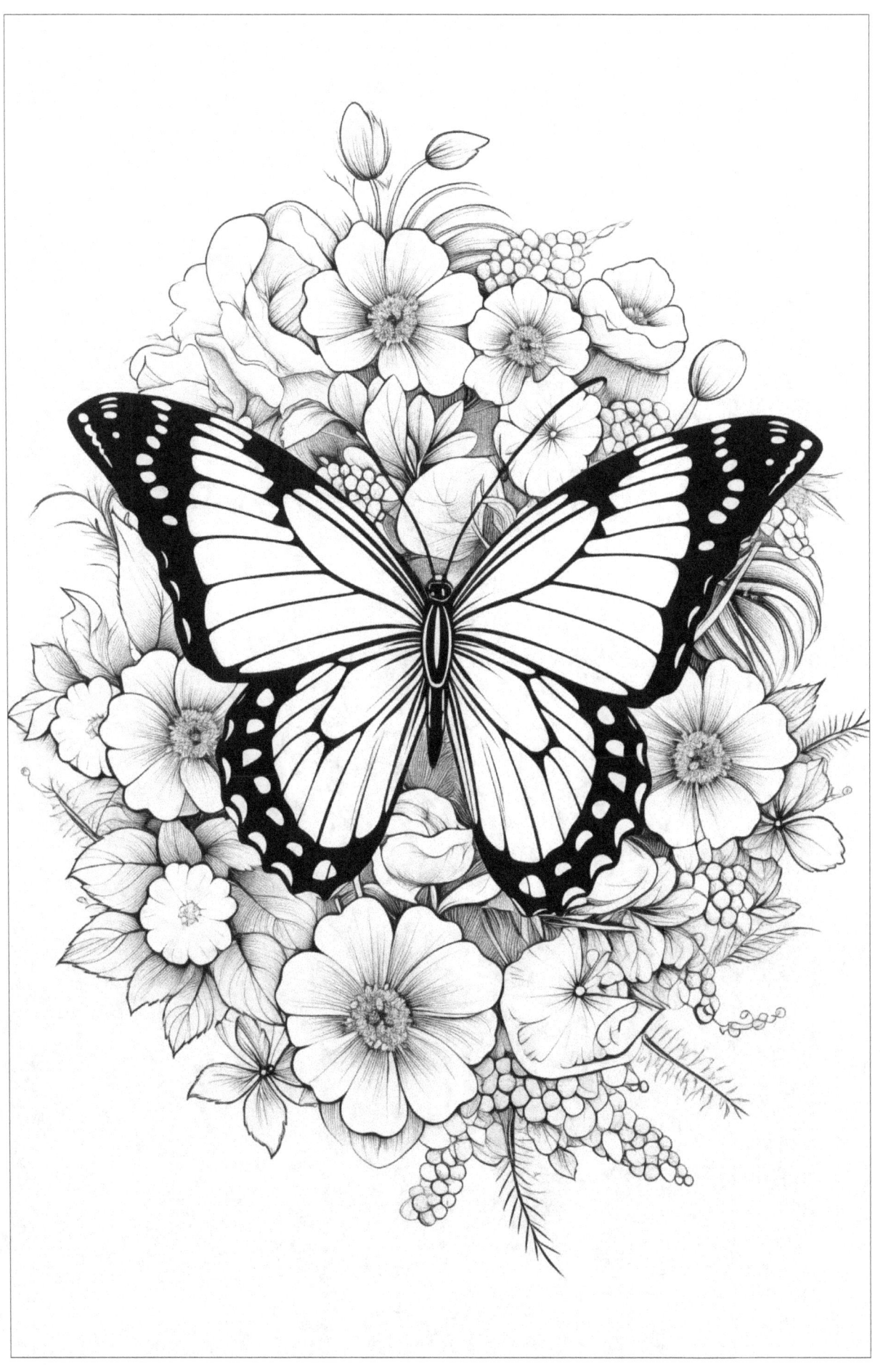

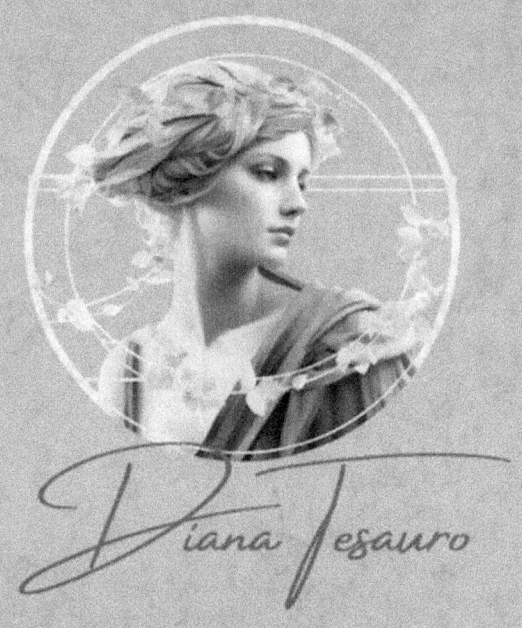

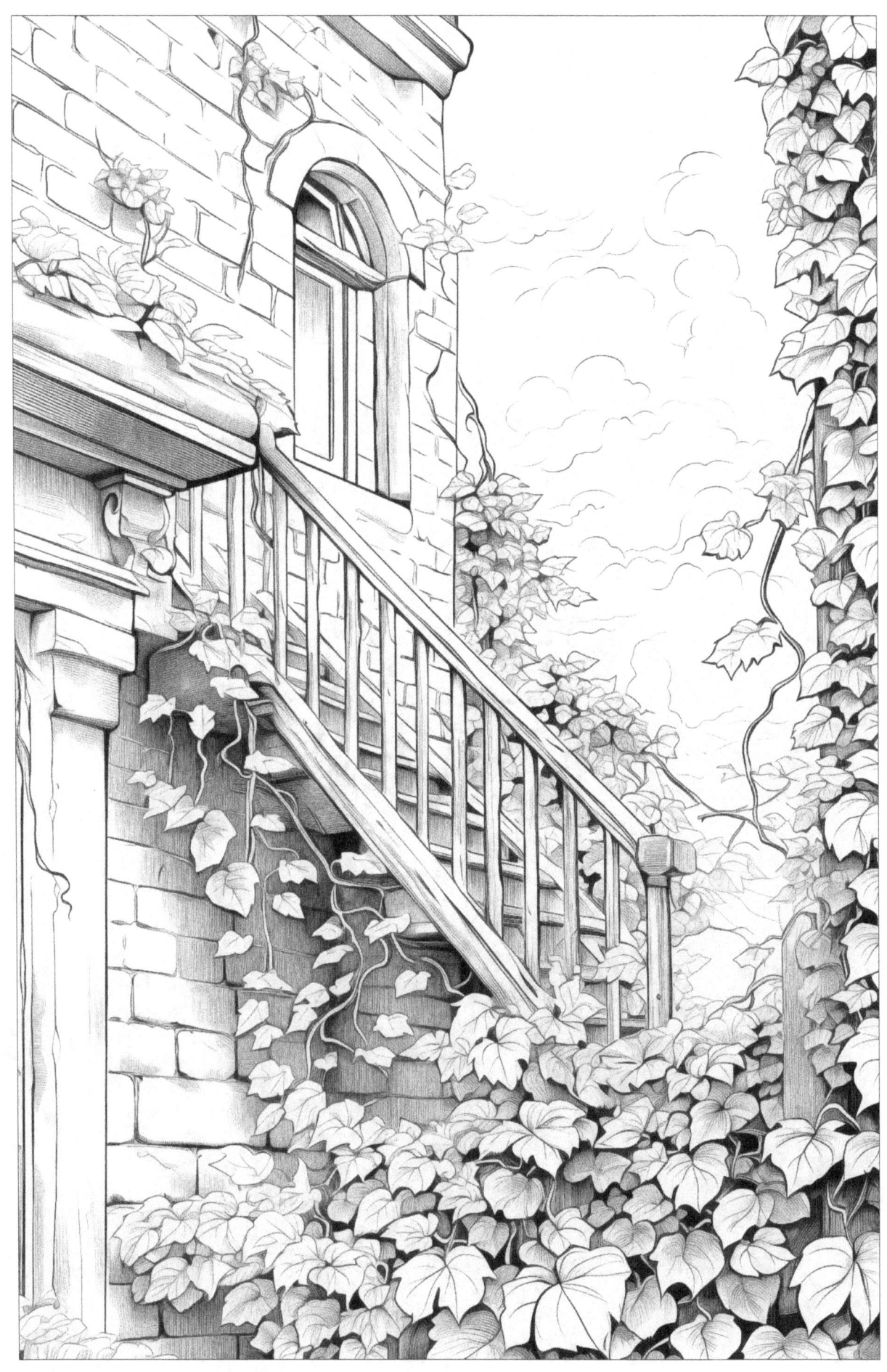

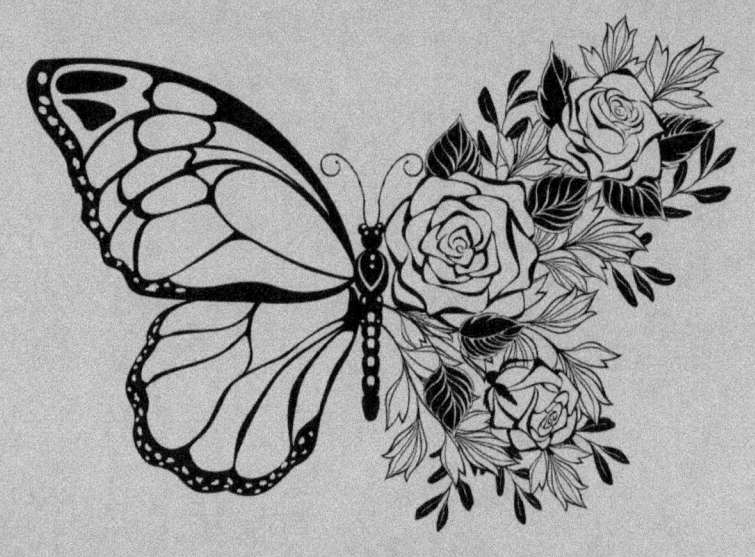

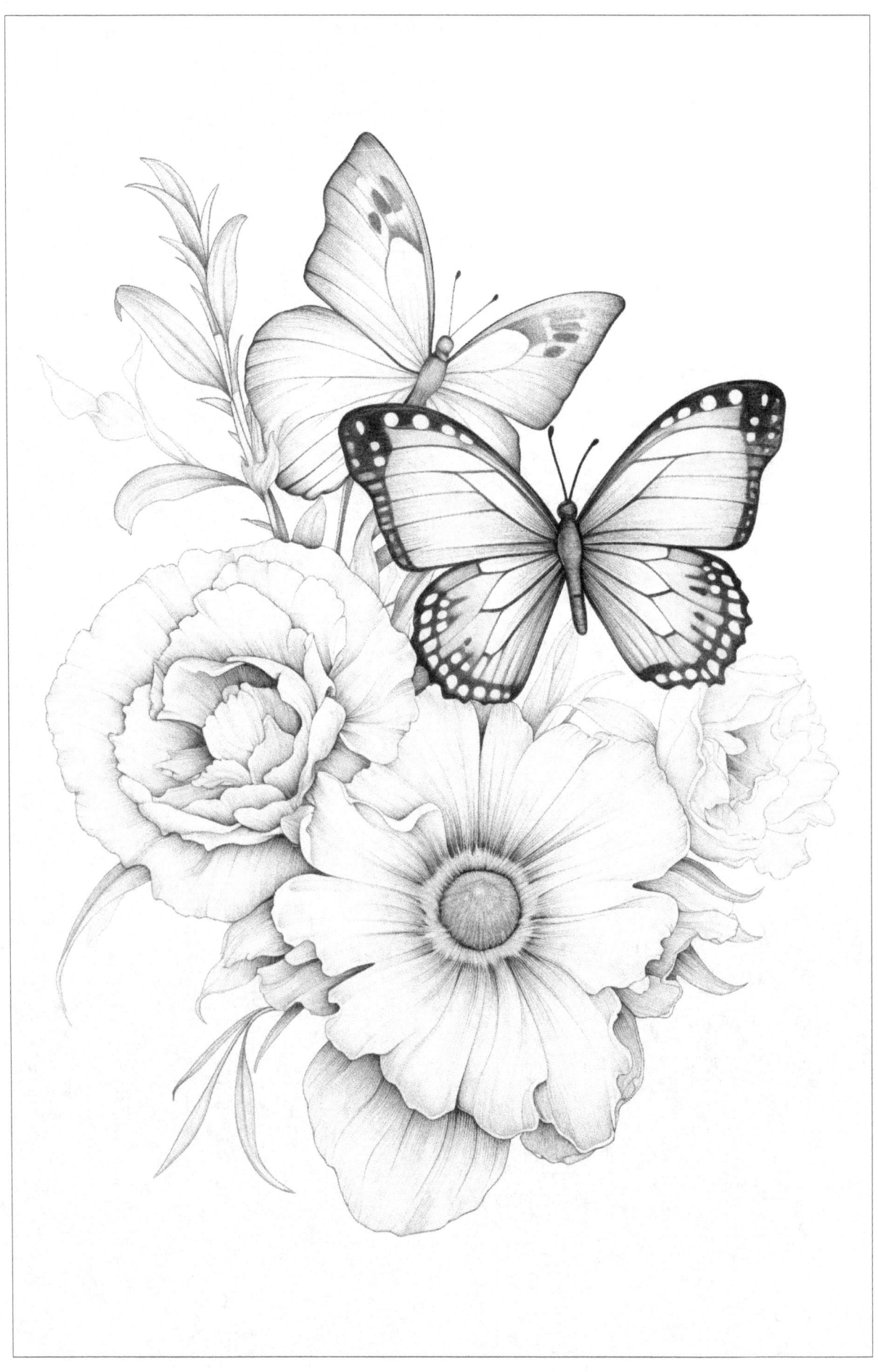

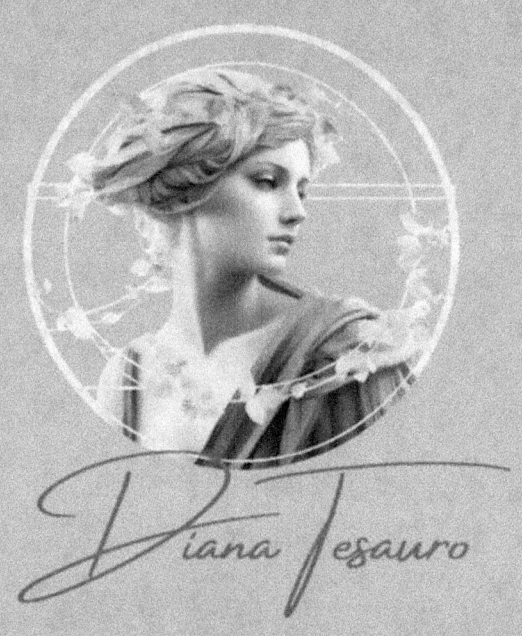

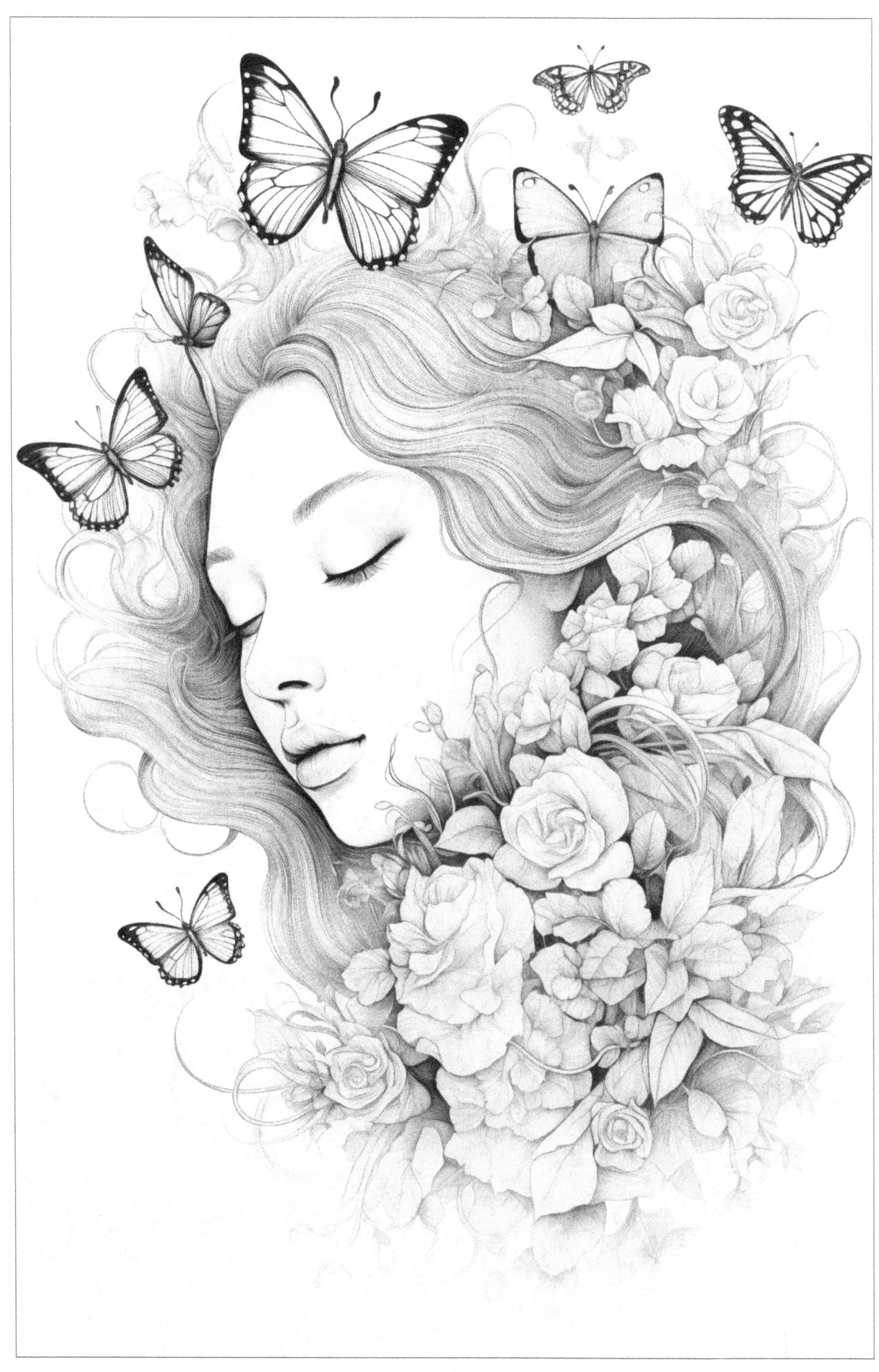

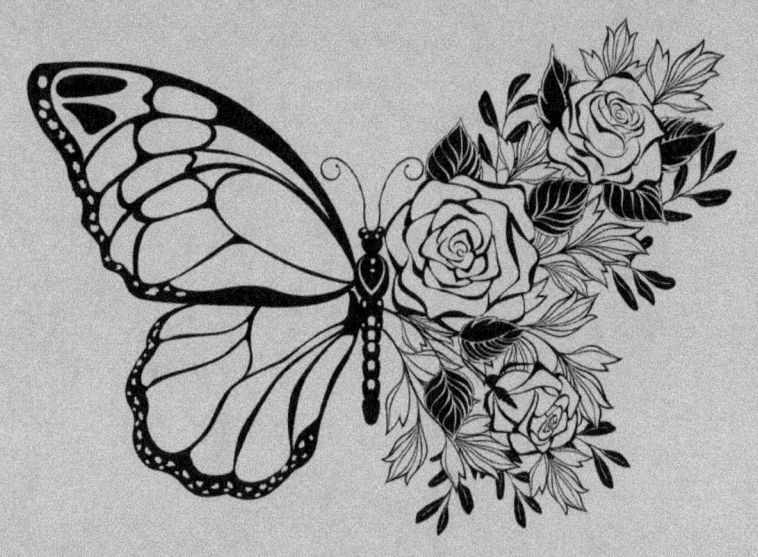

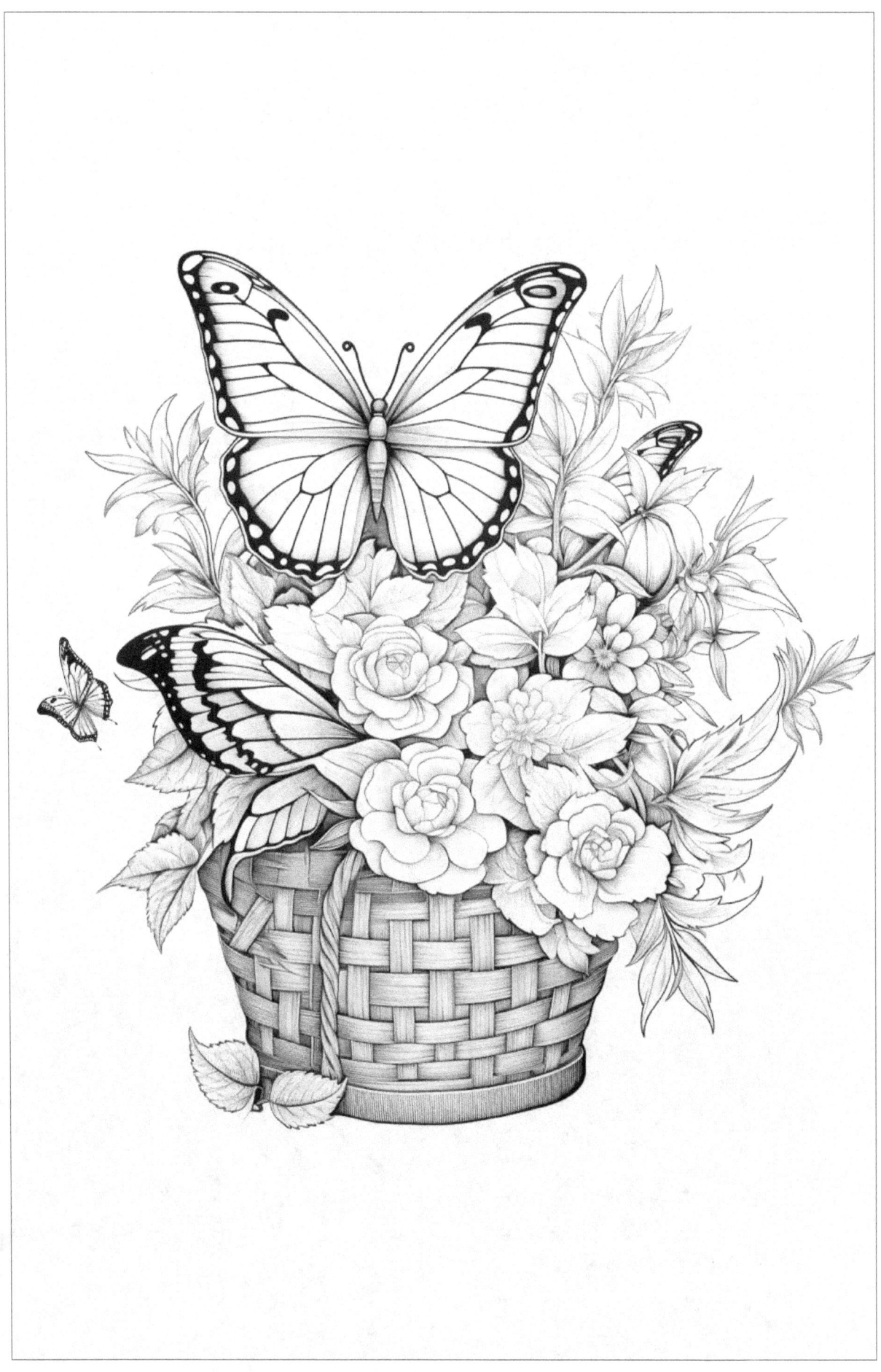

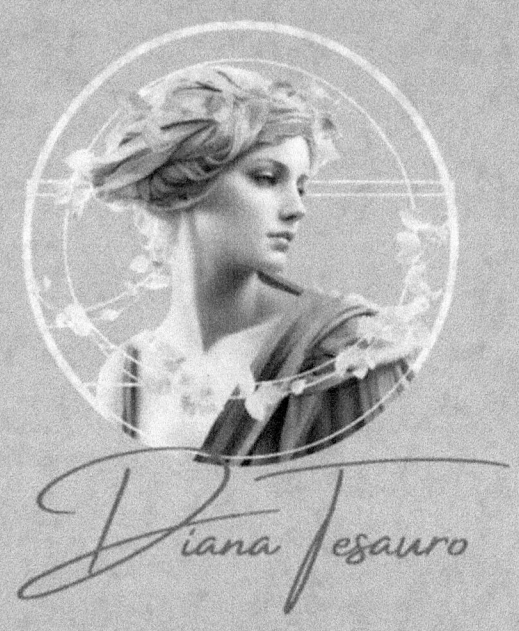

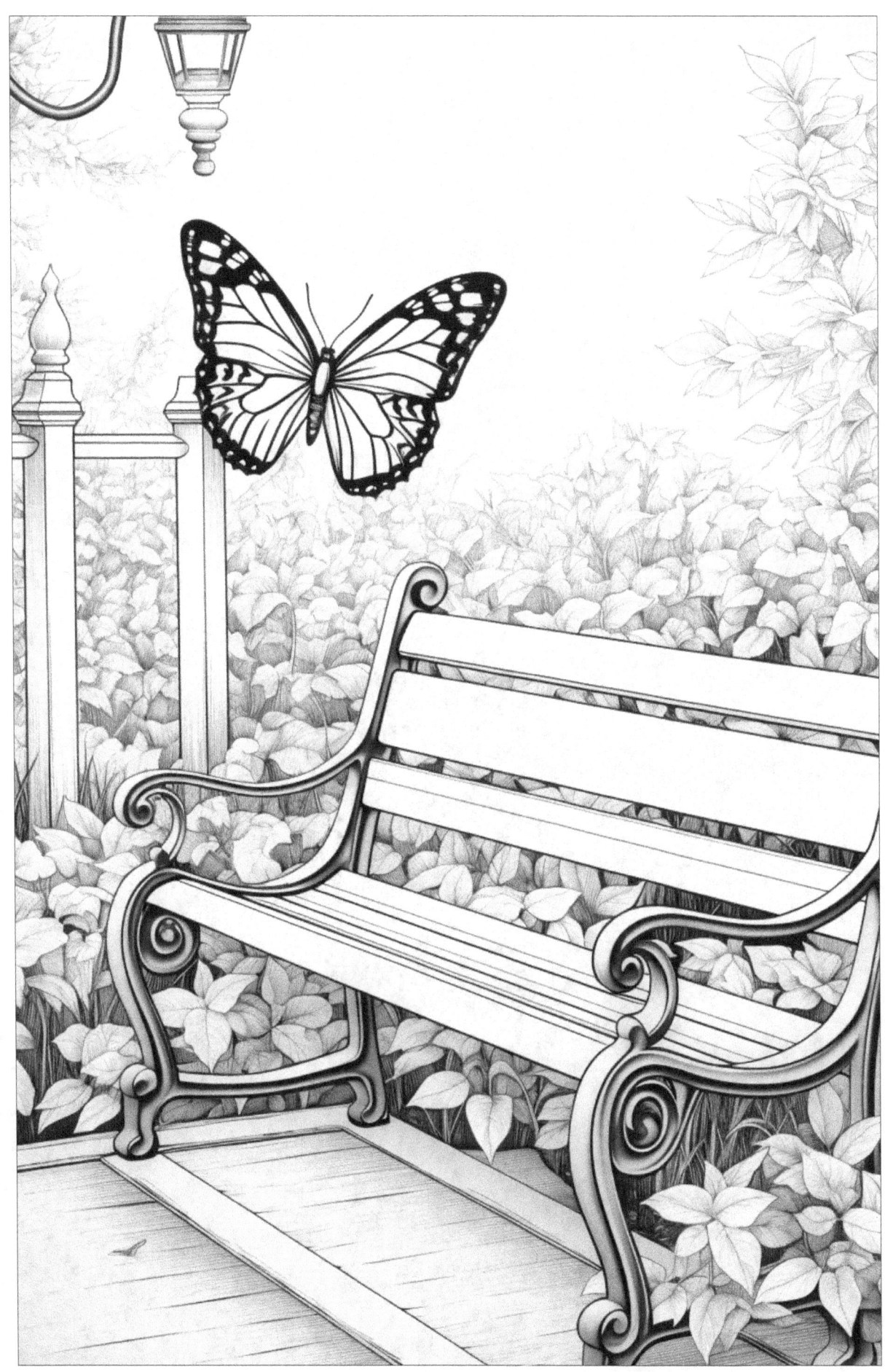

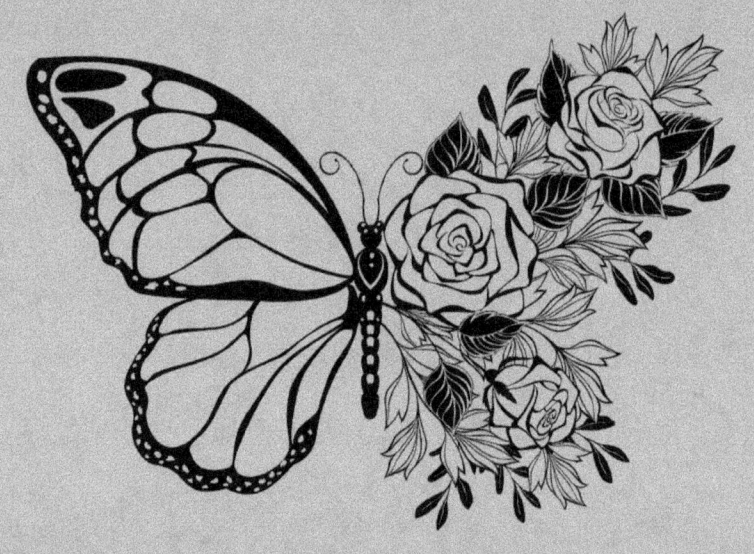

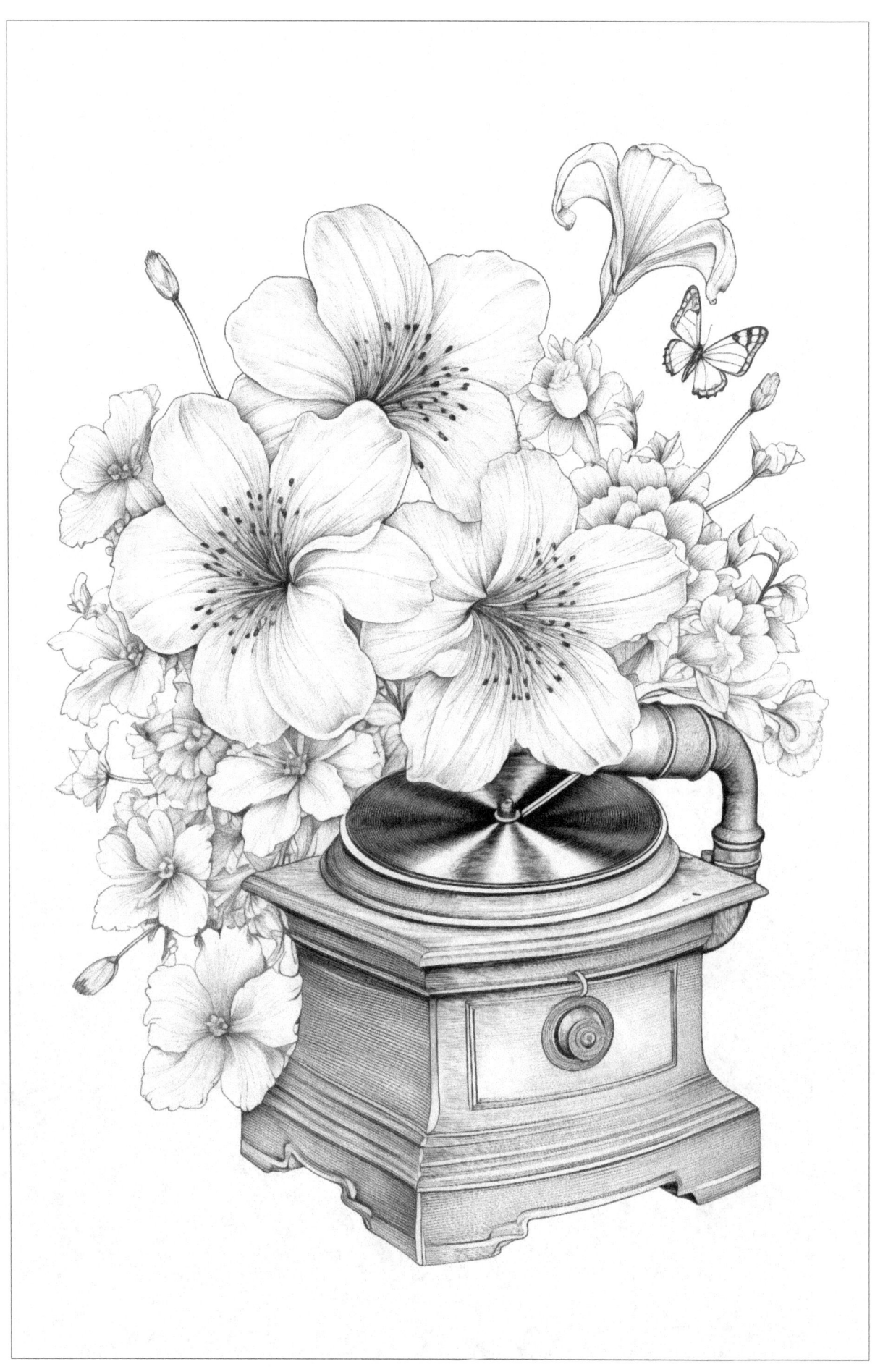

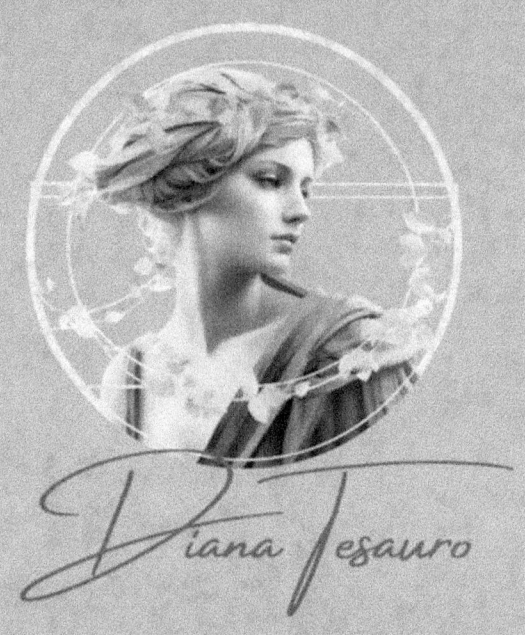

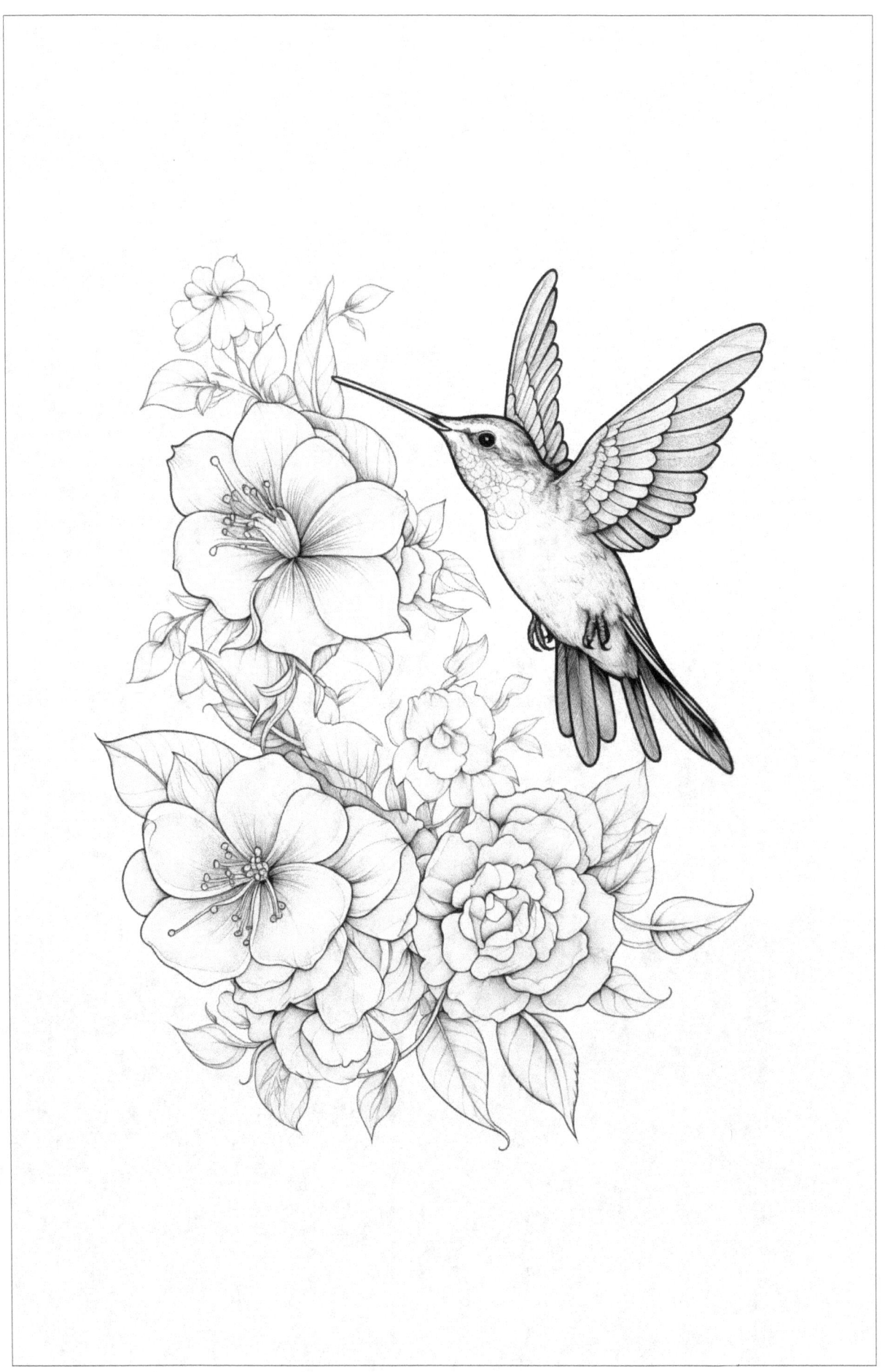

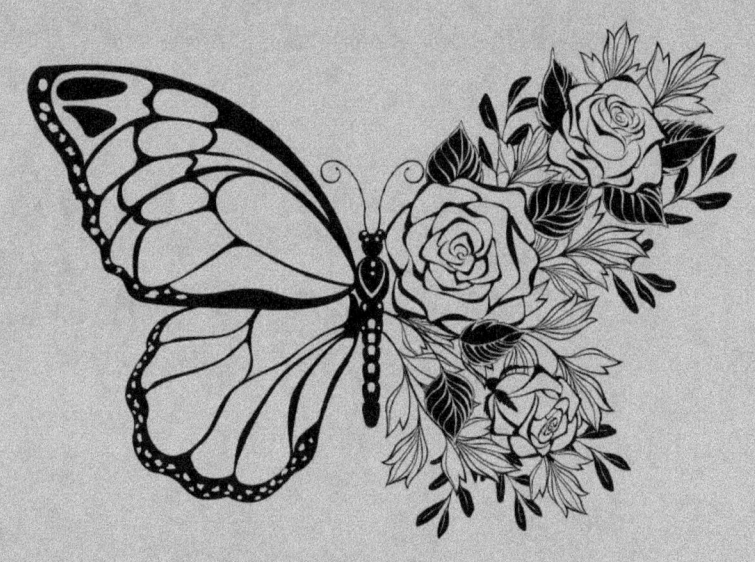

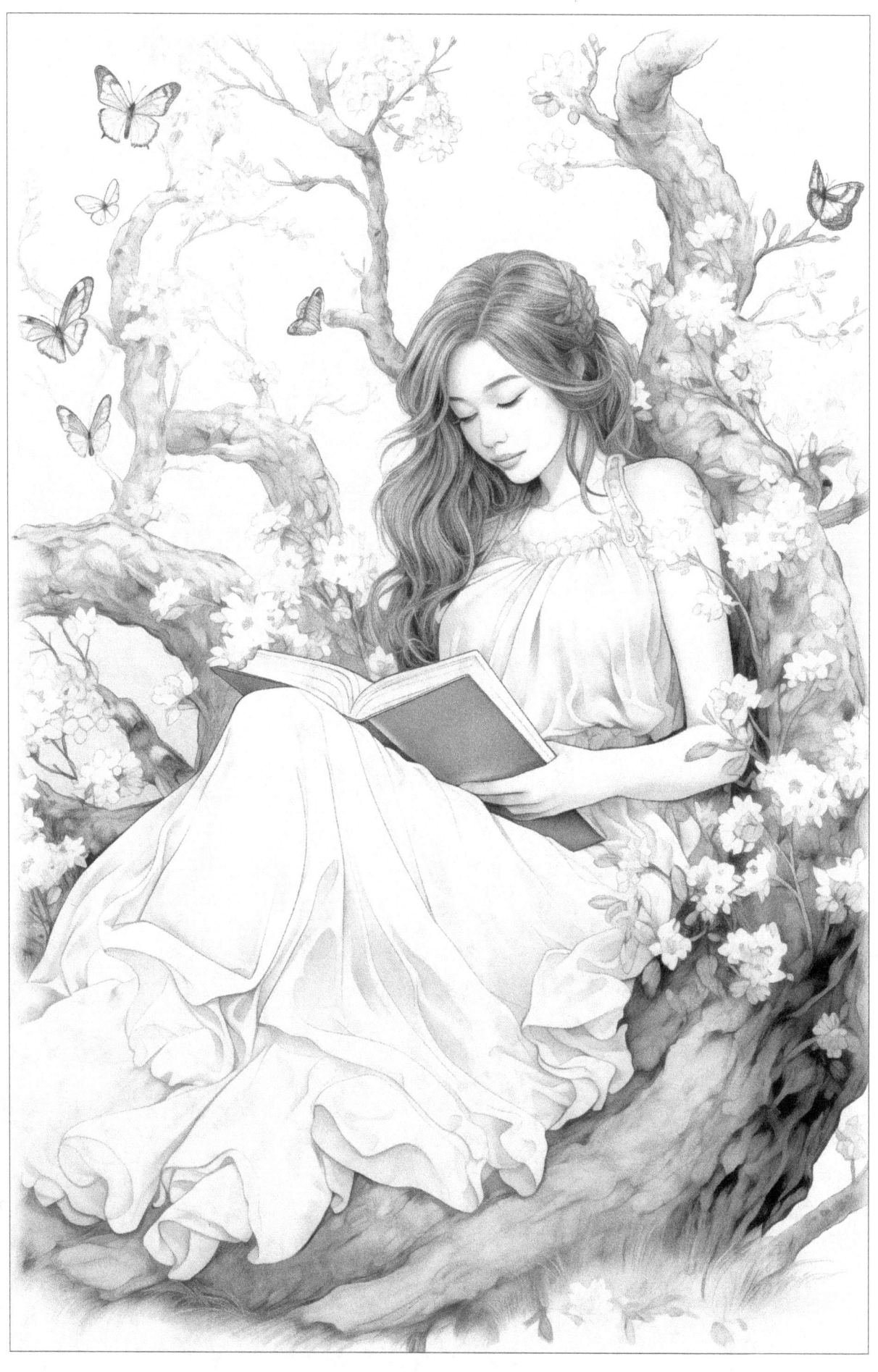

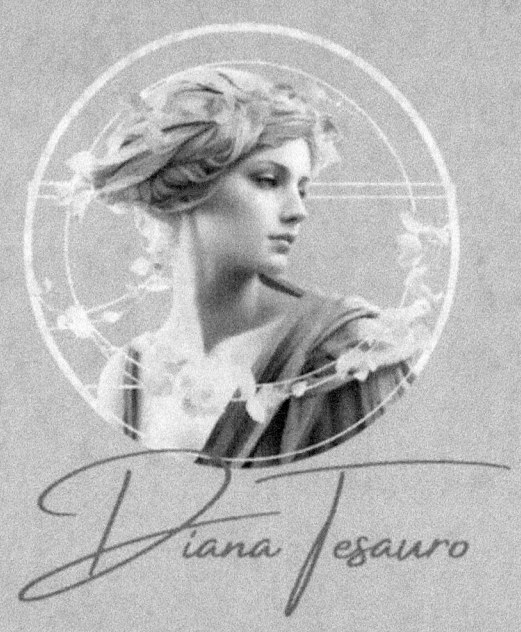

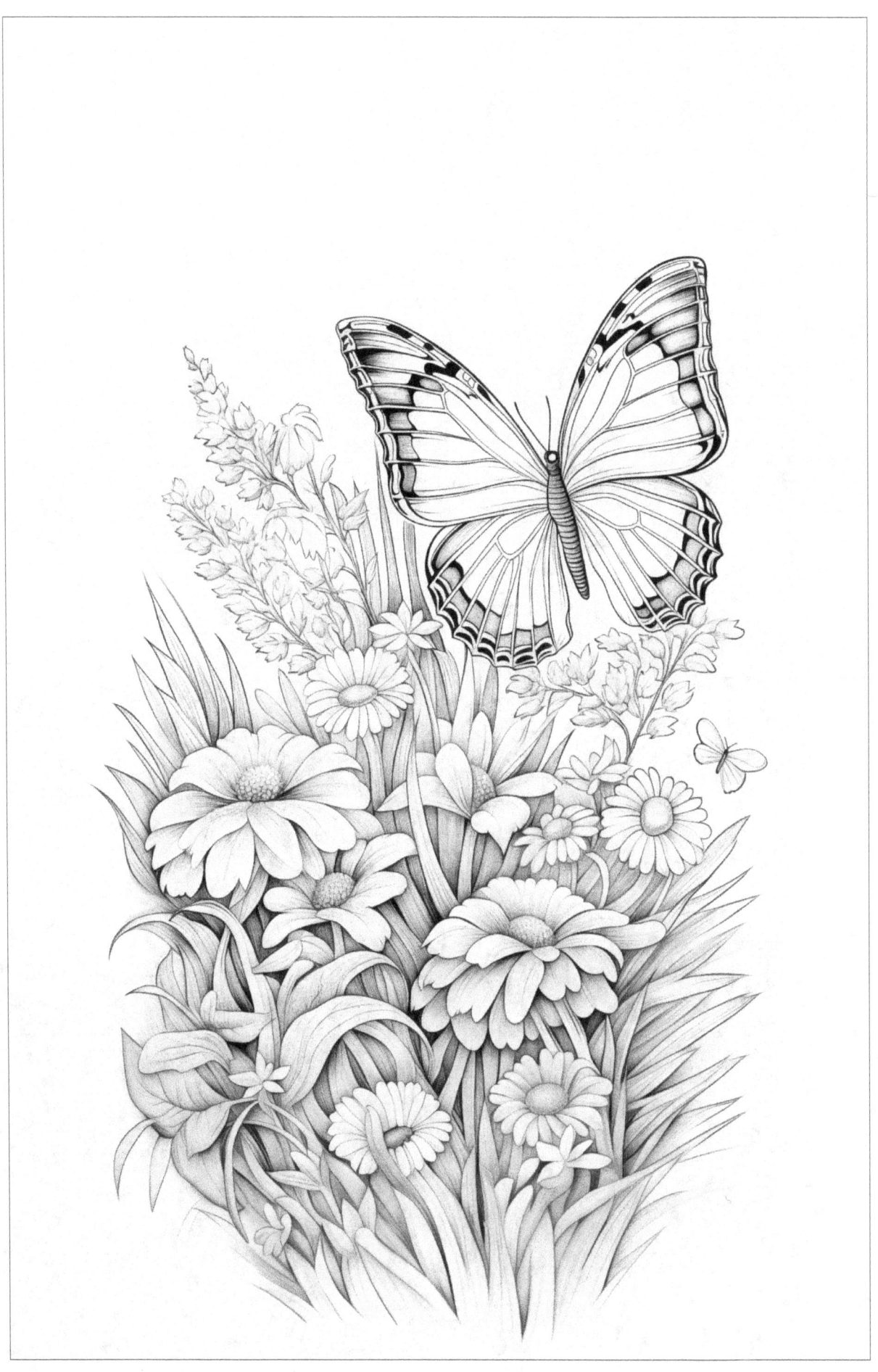

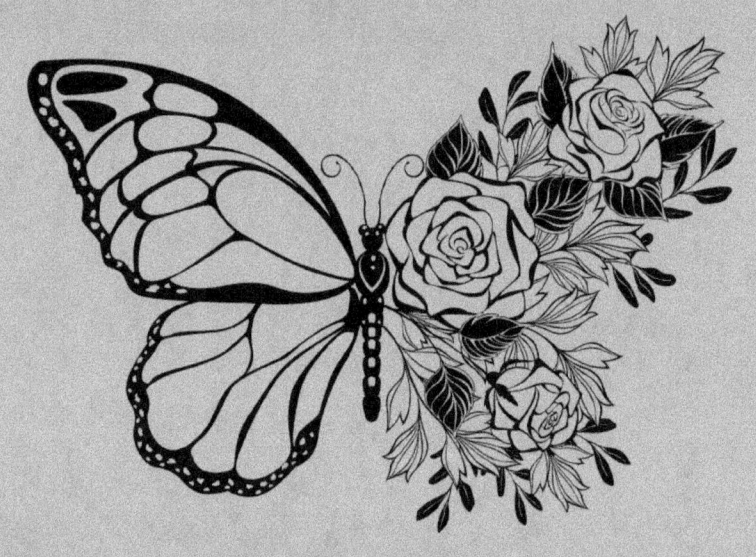

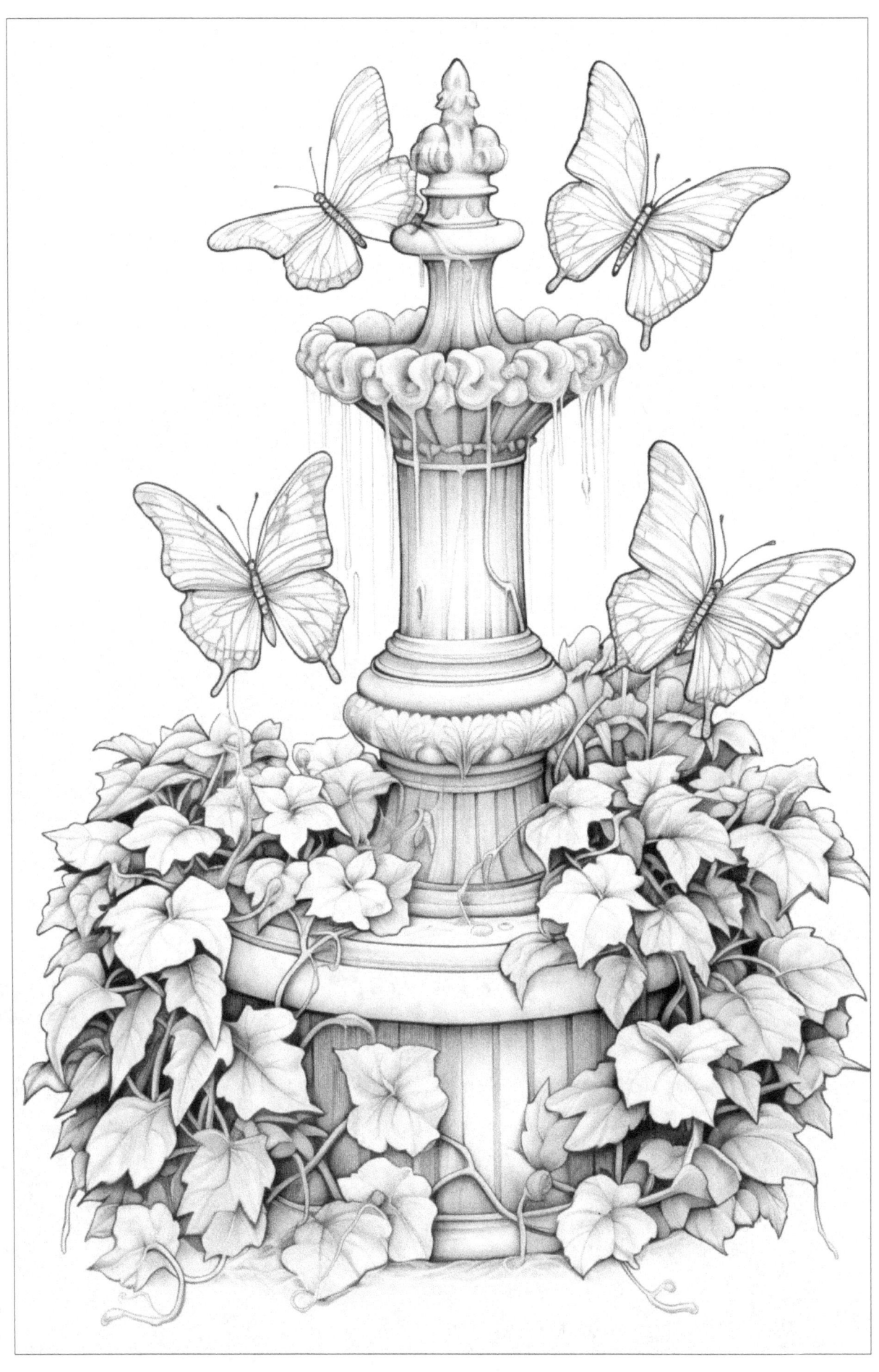

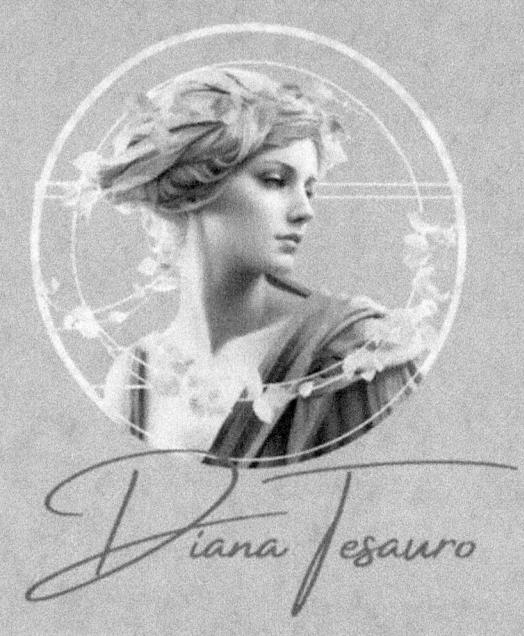

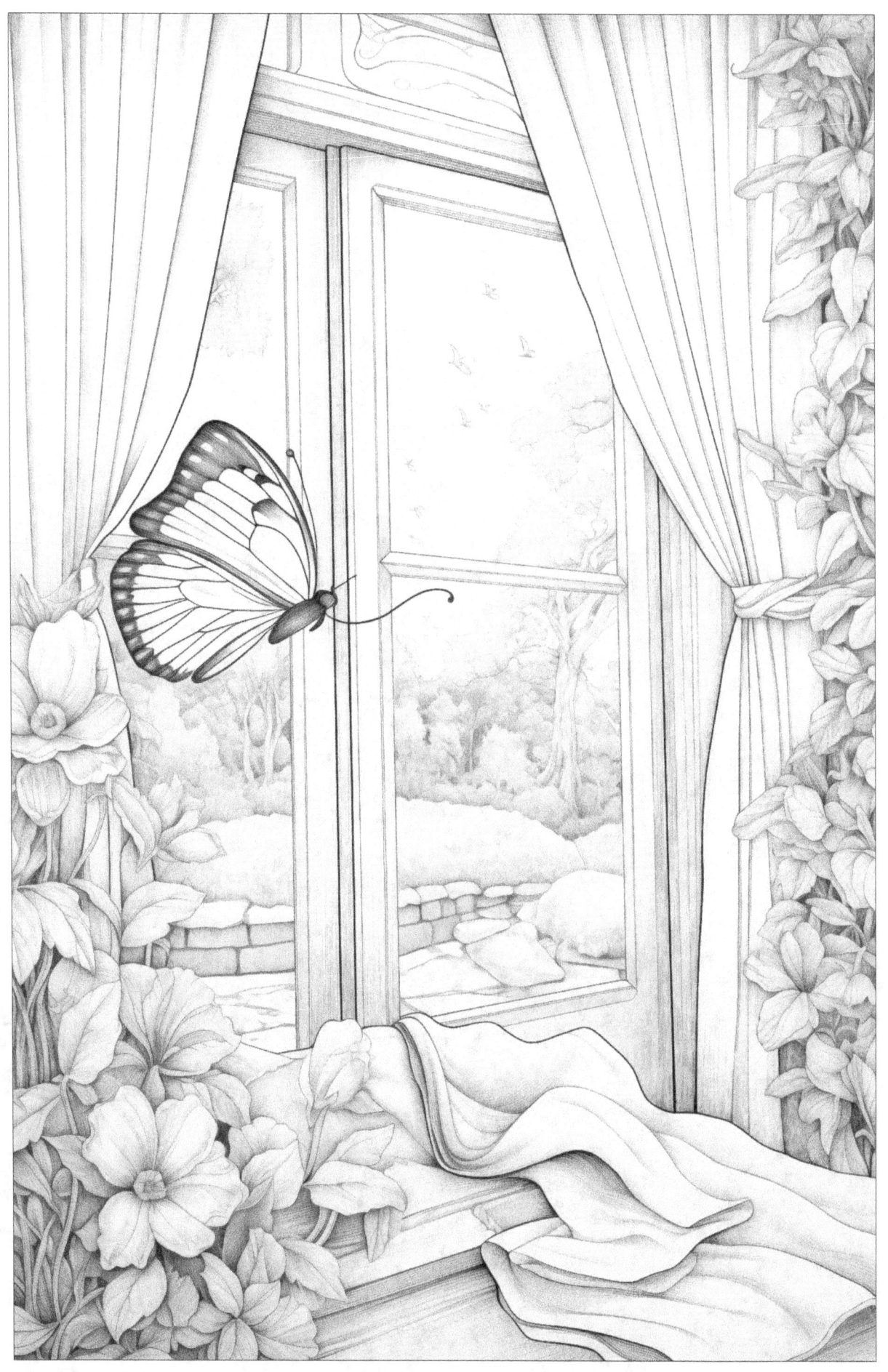

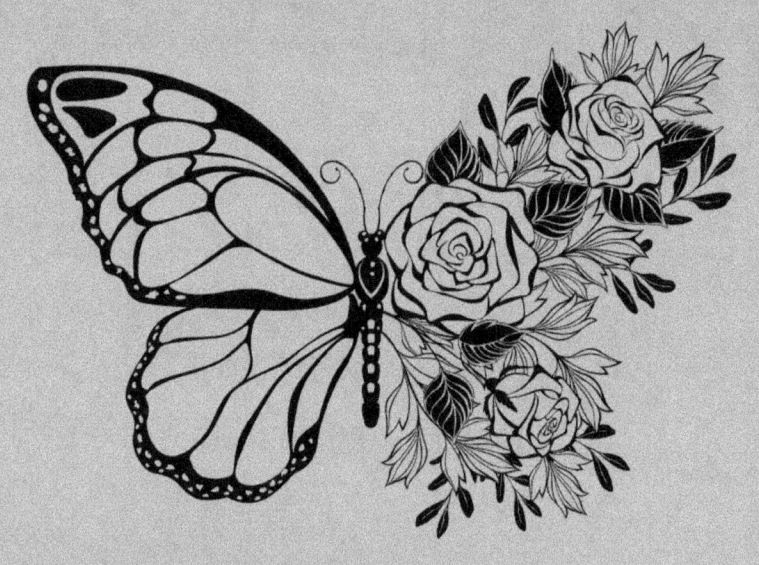

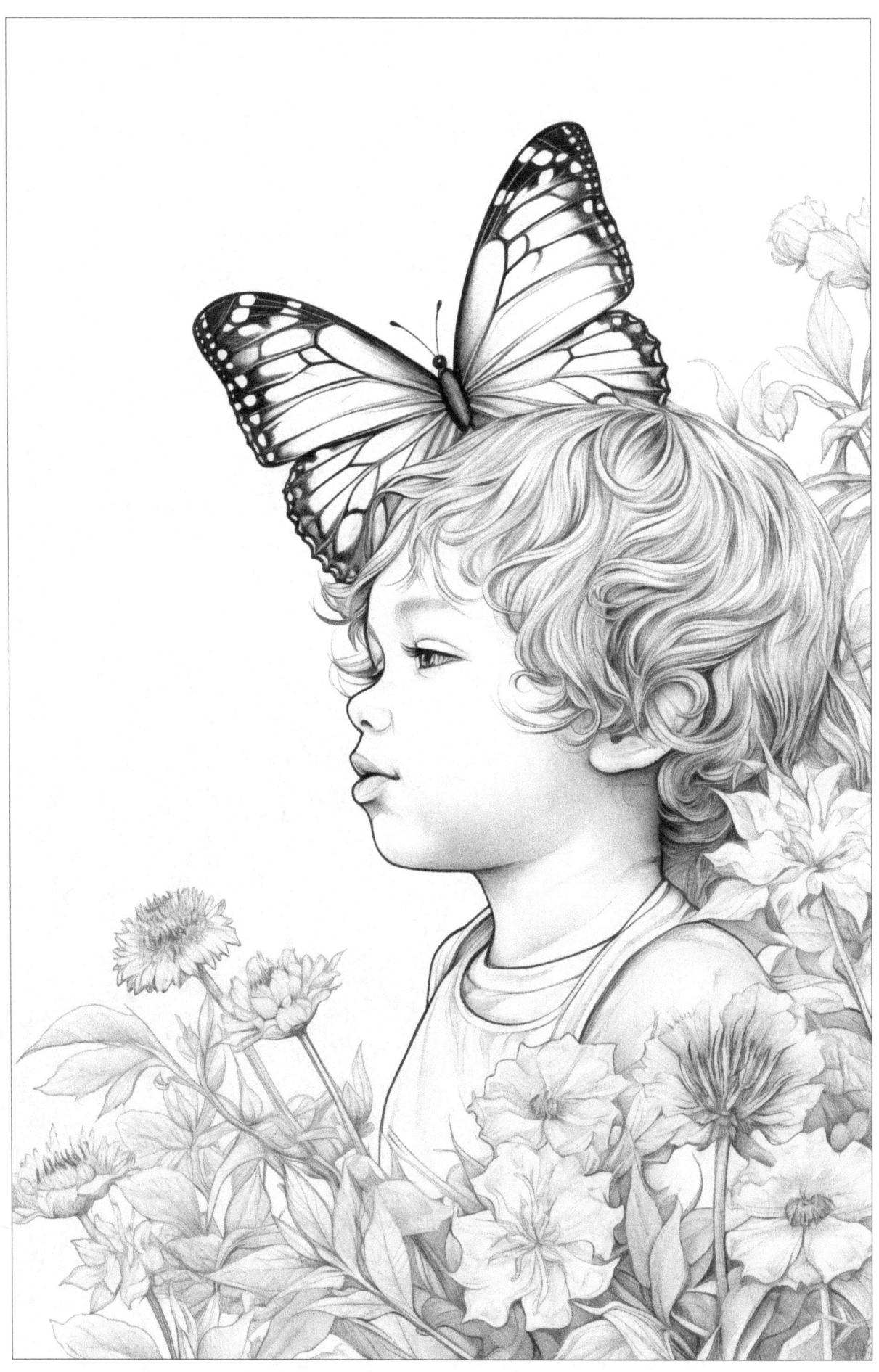

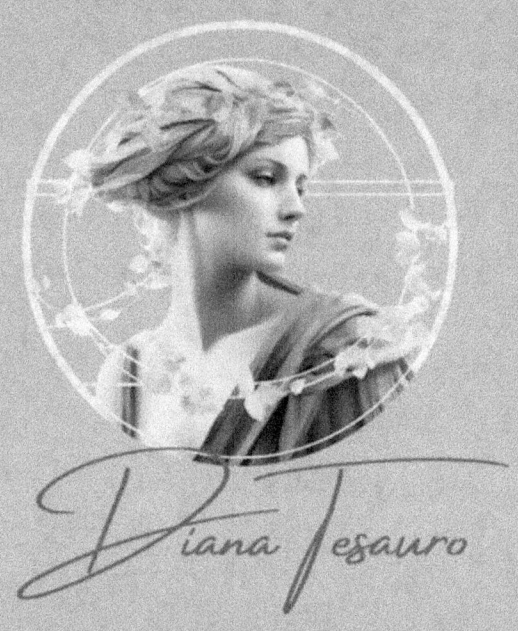

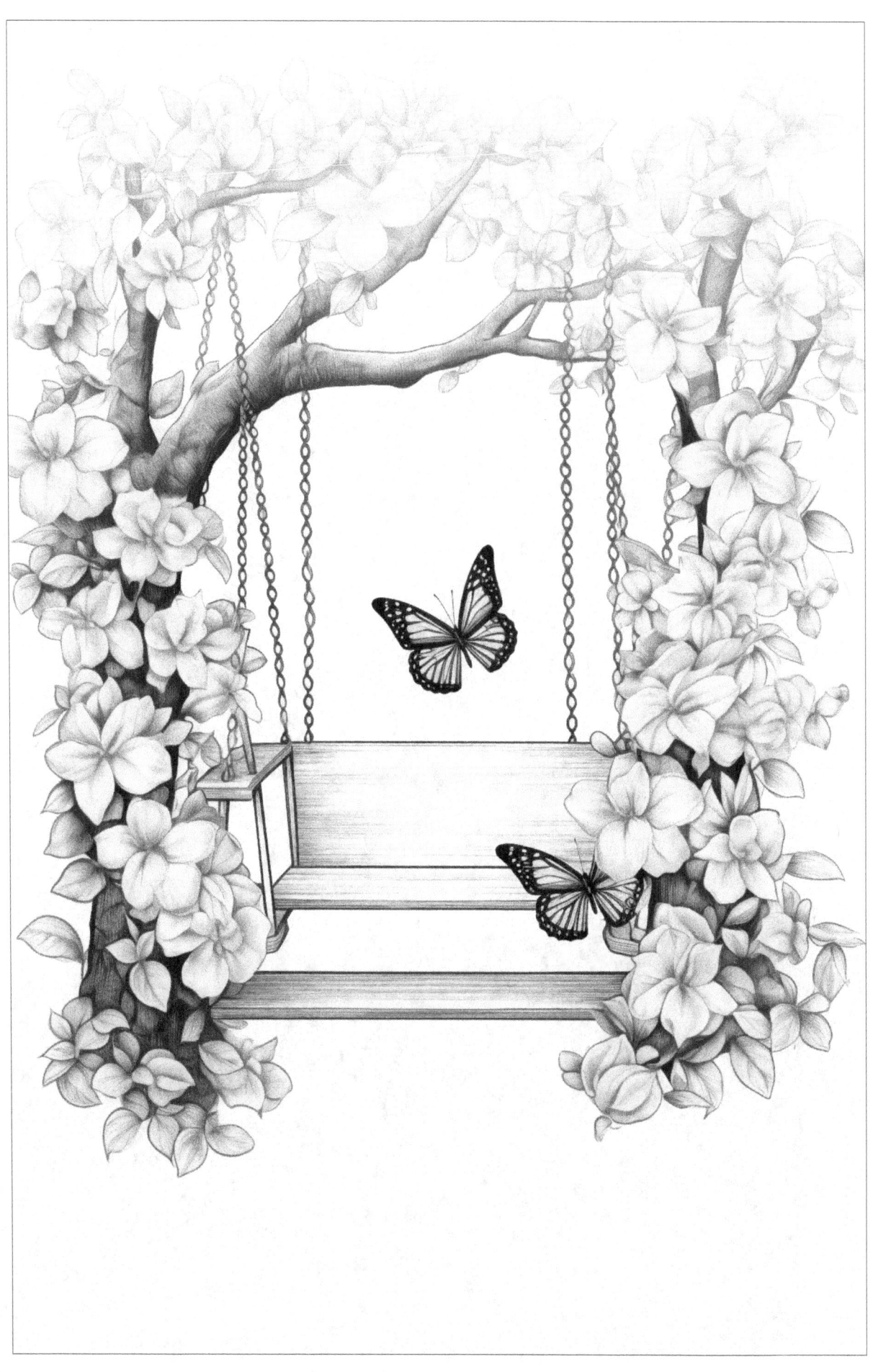

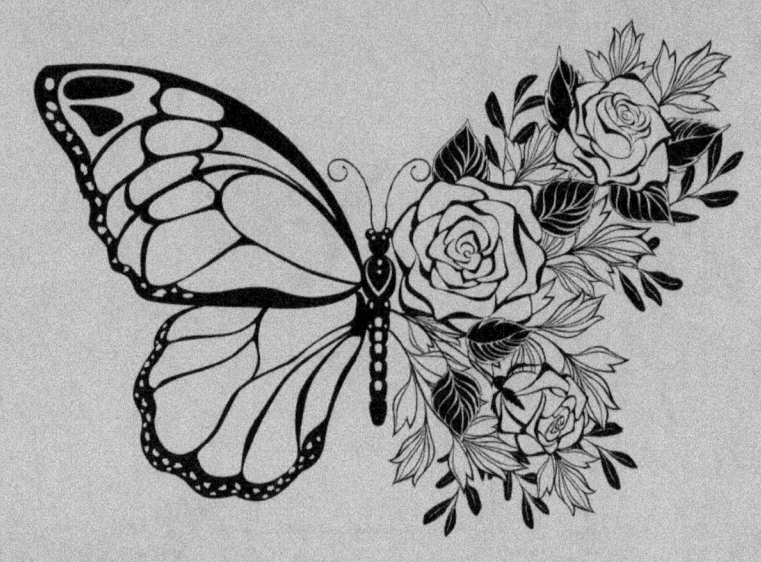

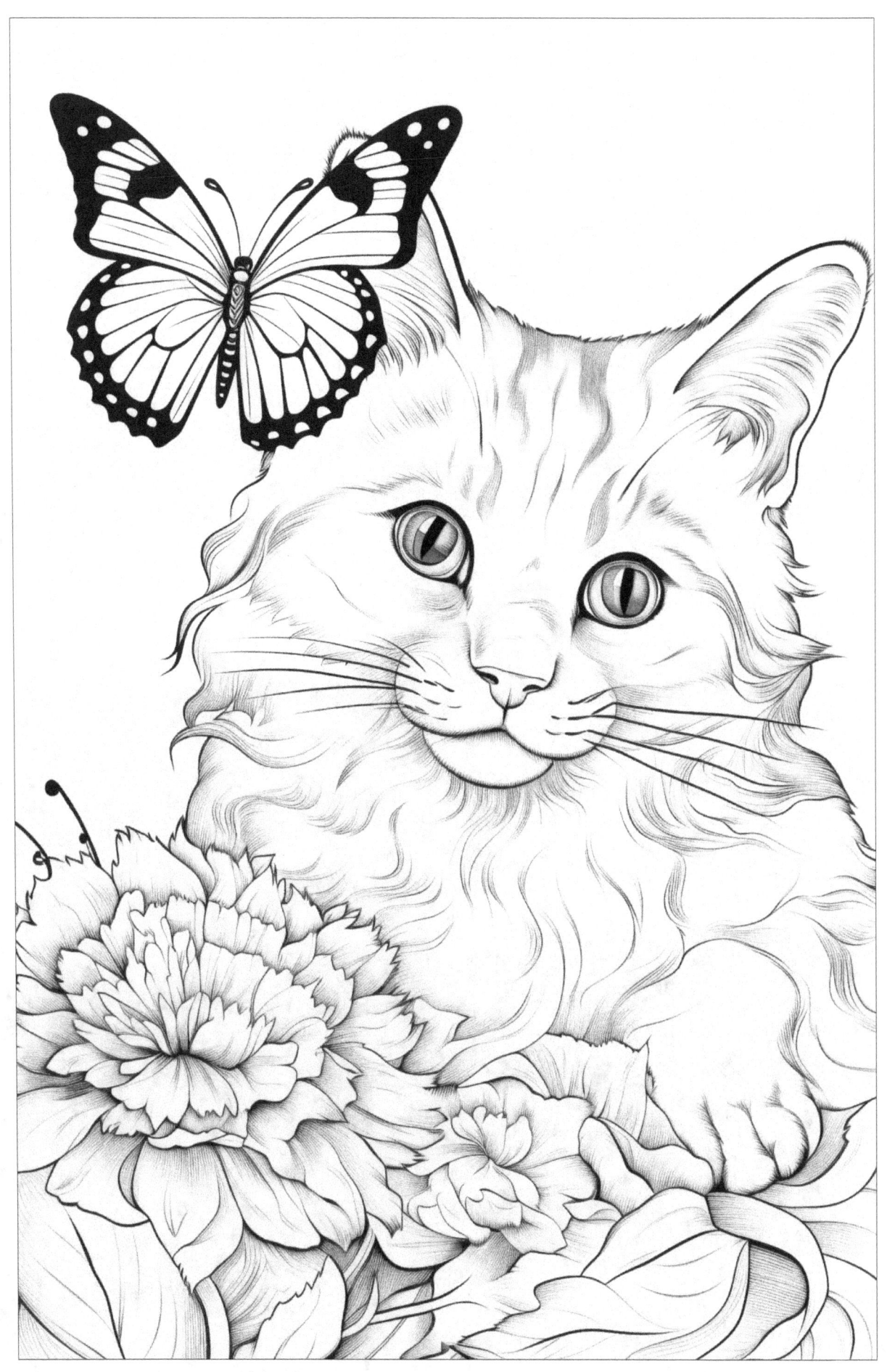

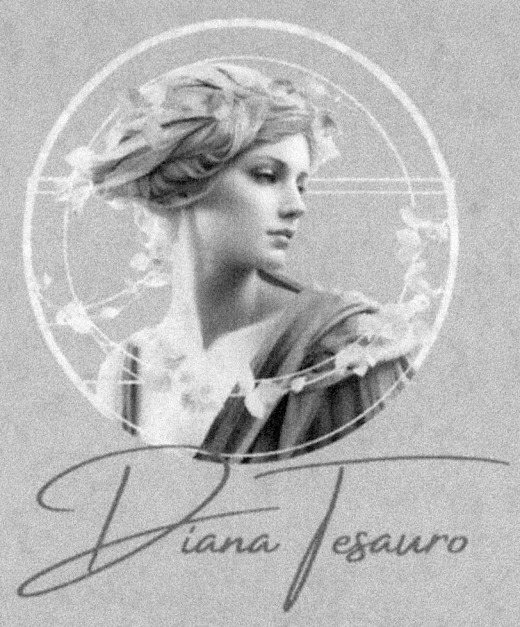

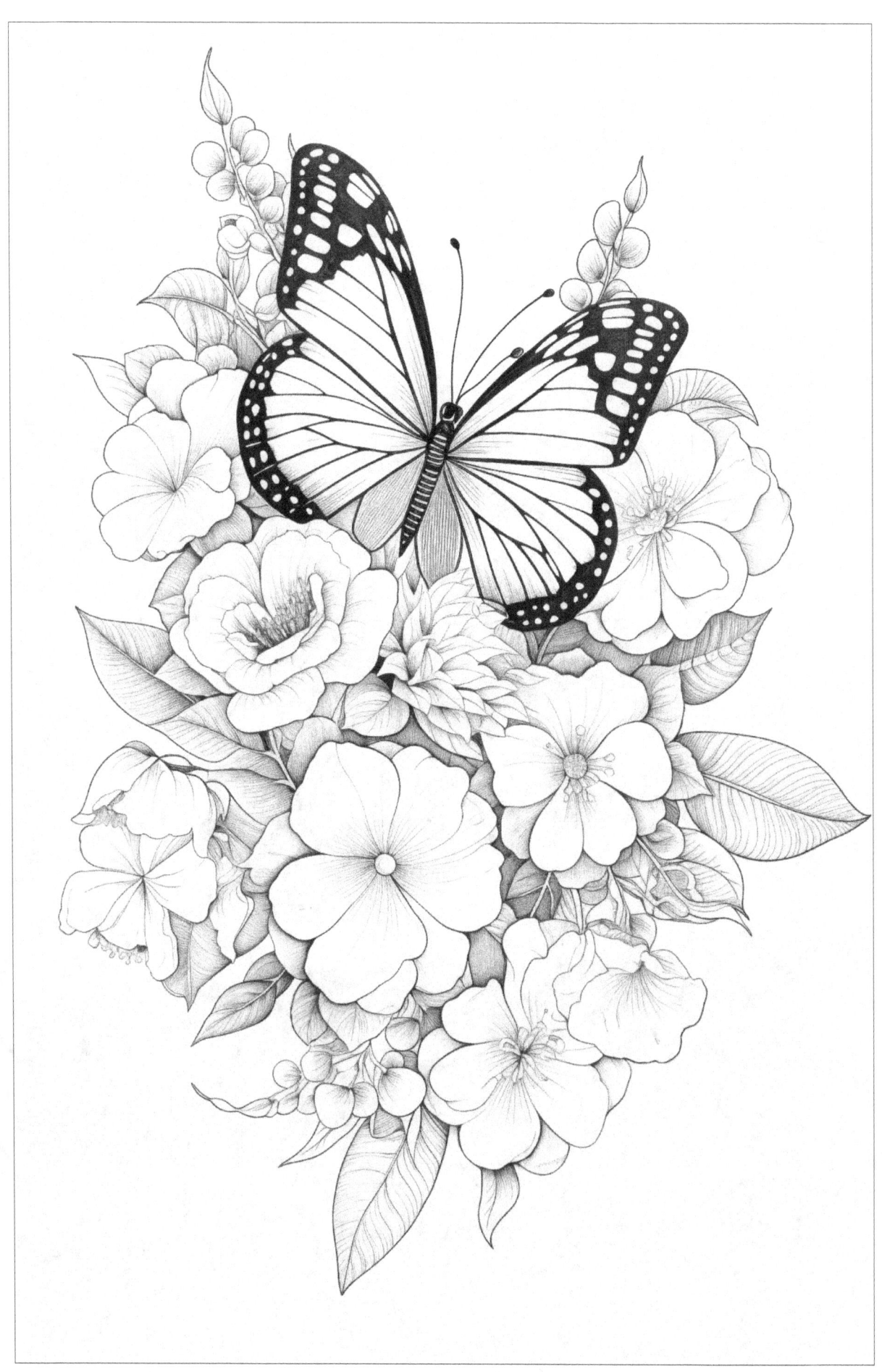

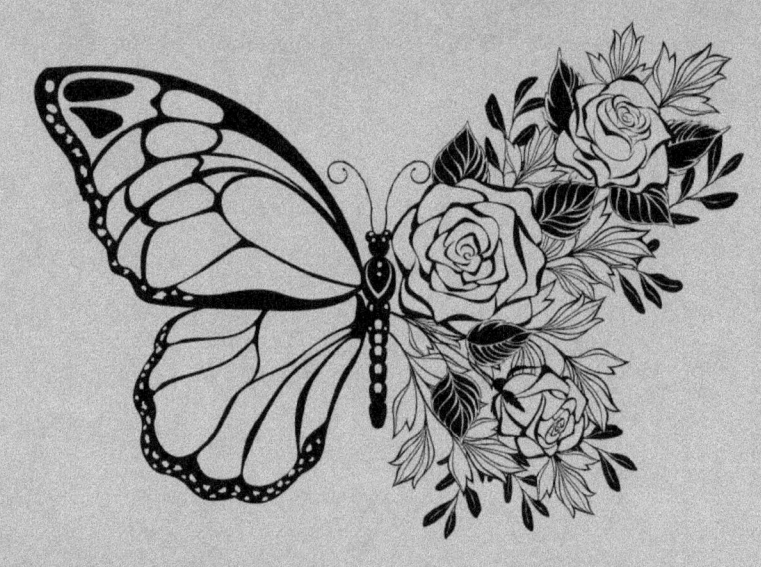

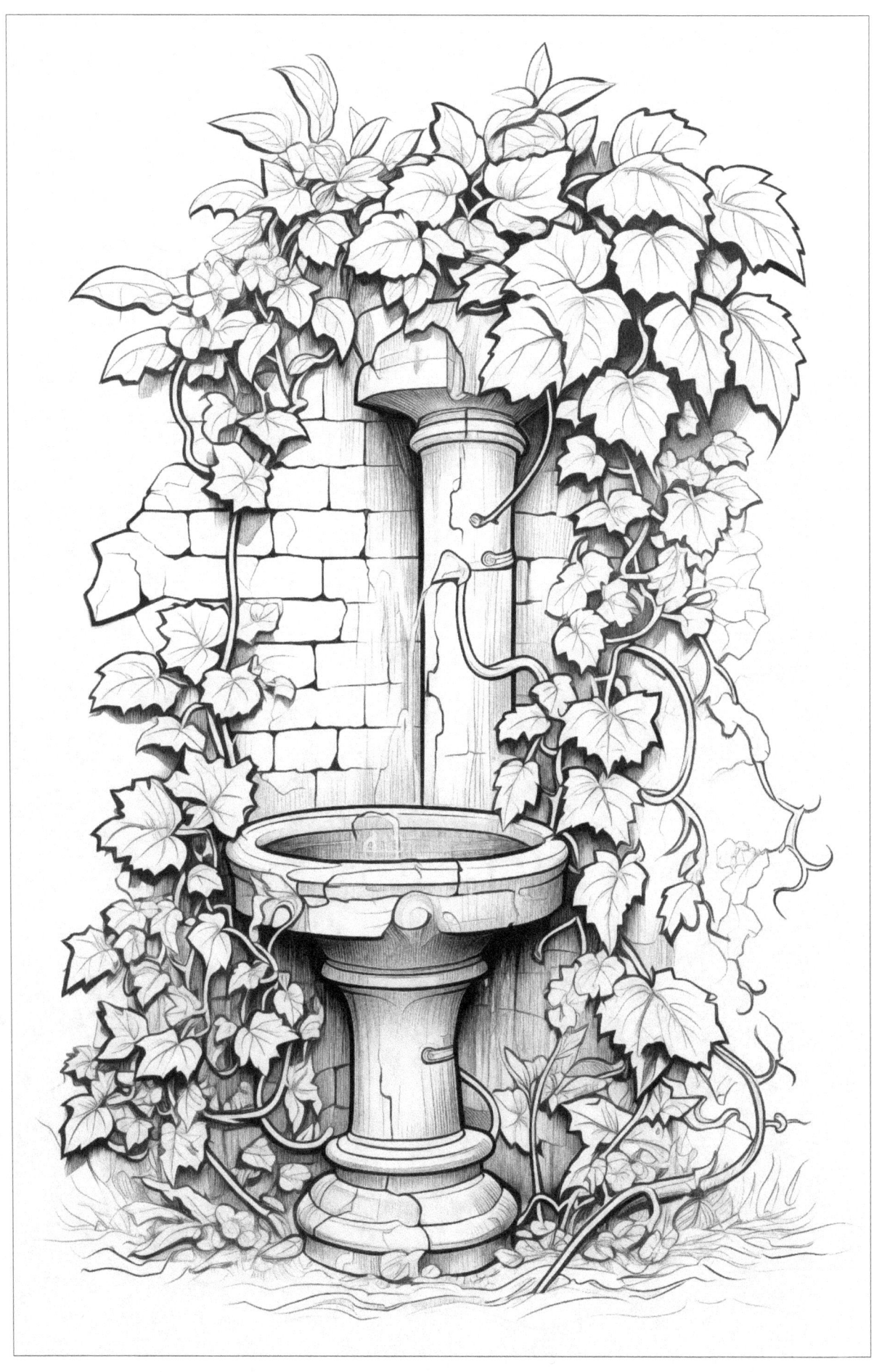

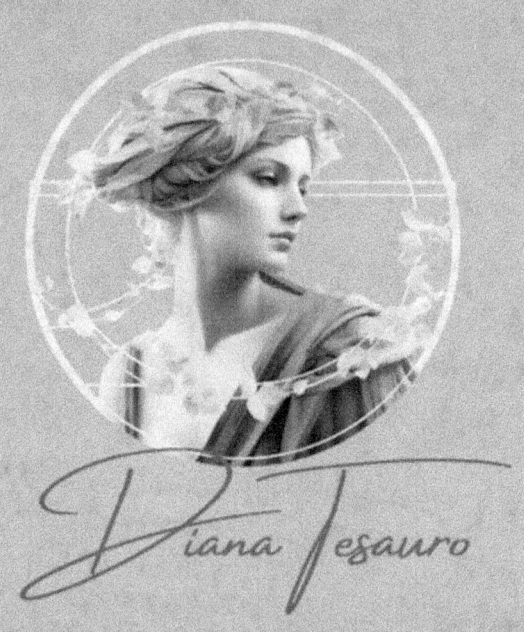

Diana Tesauro

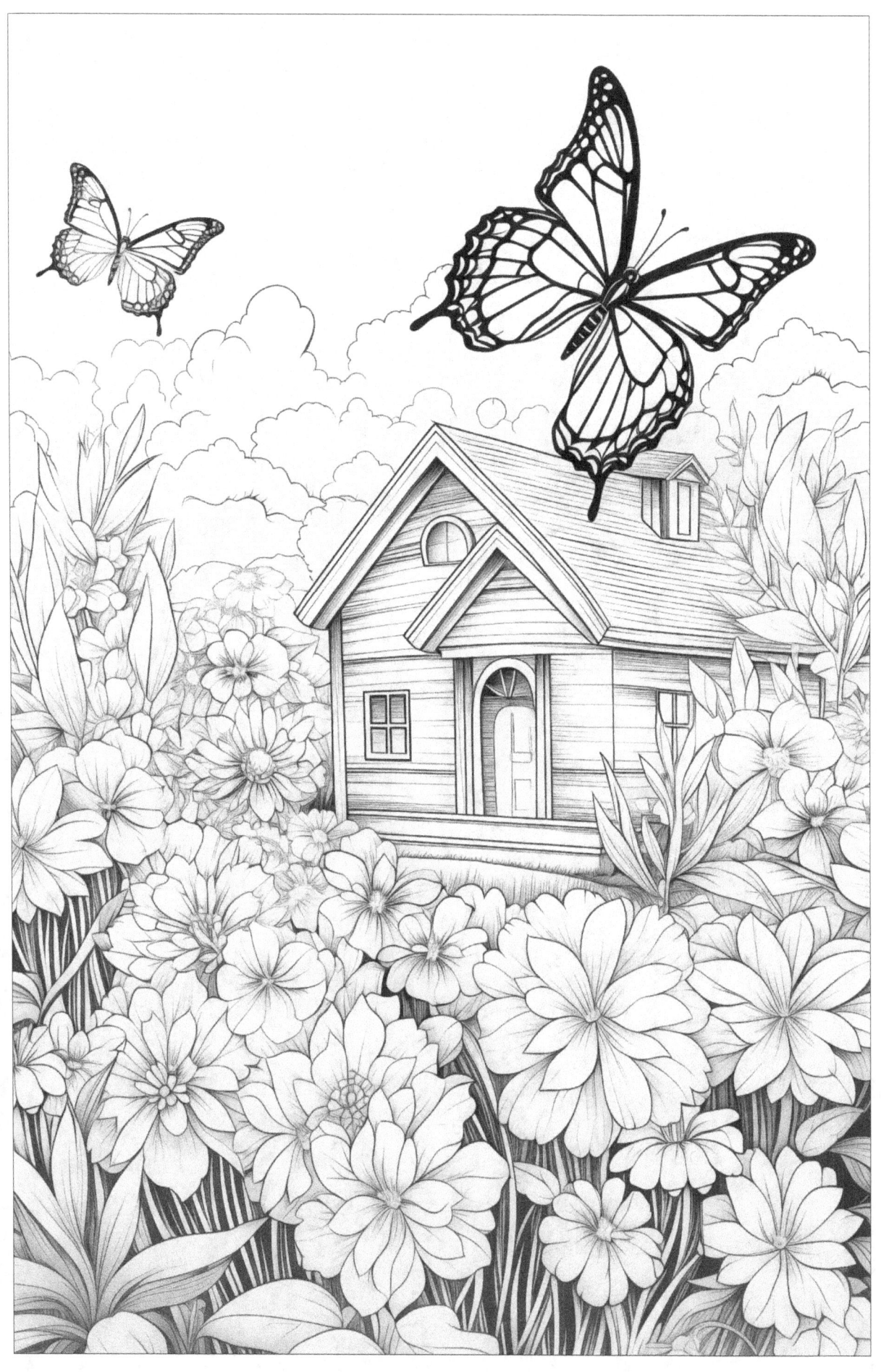

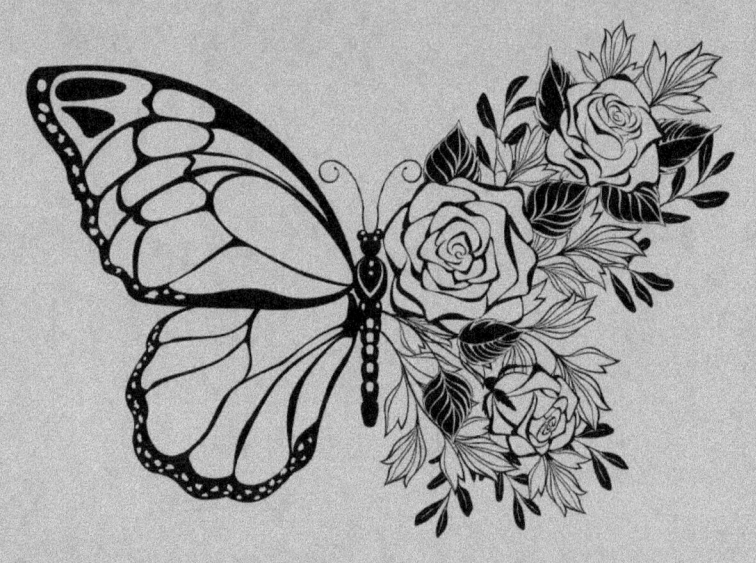

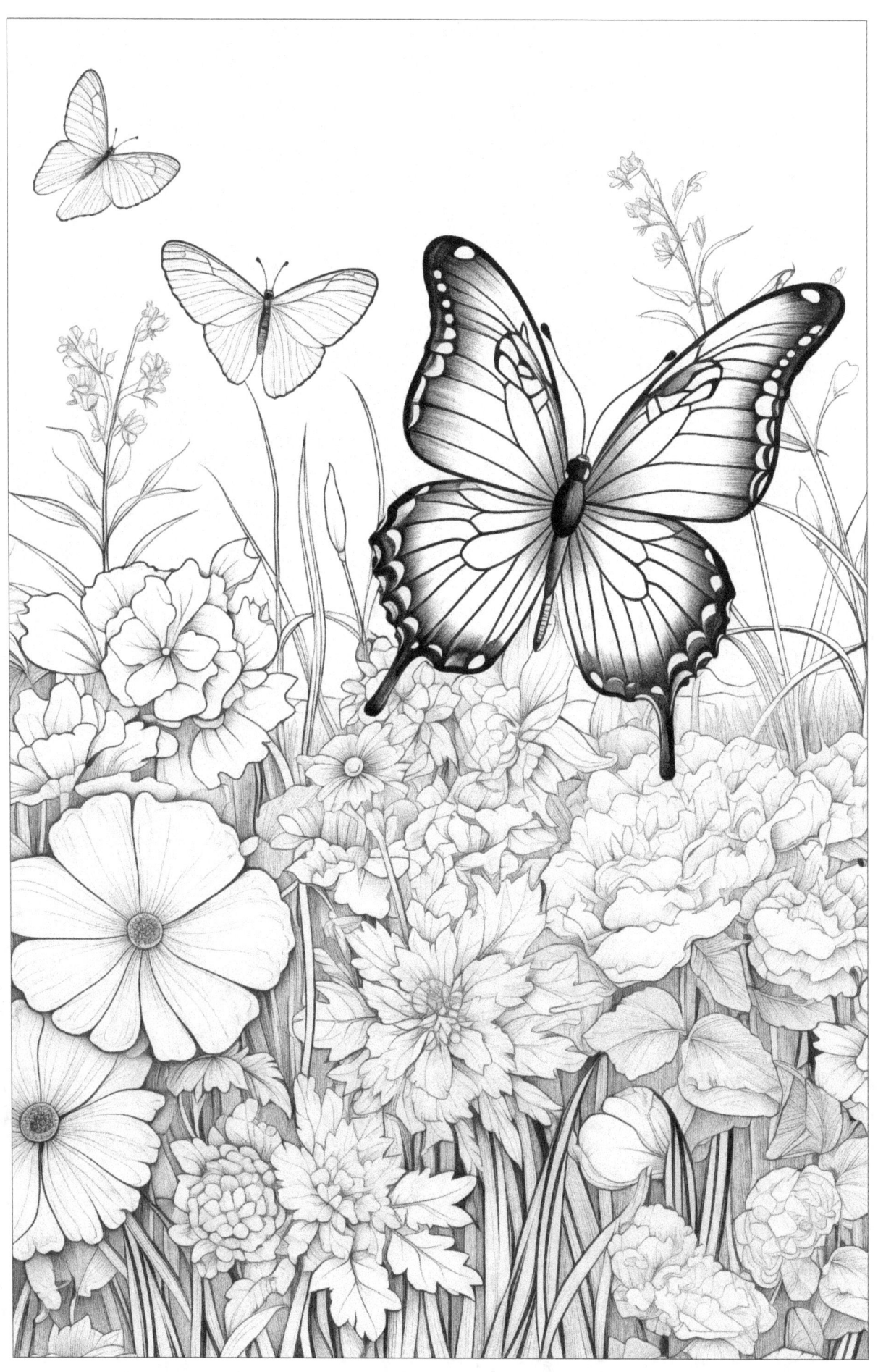

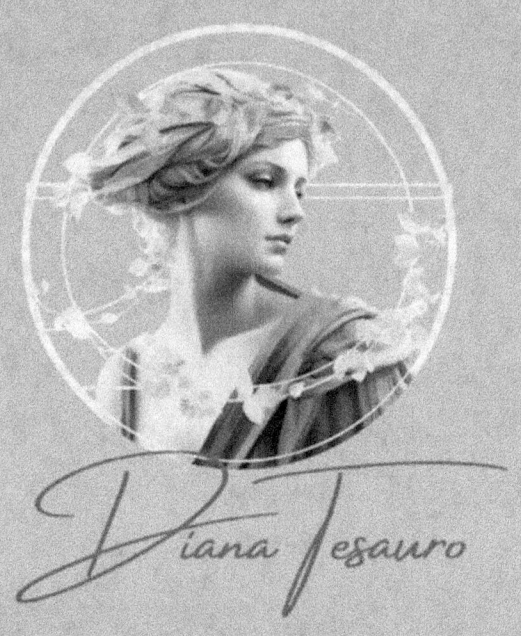

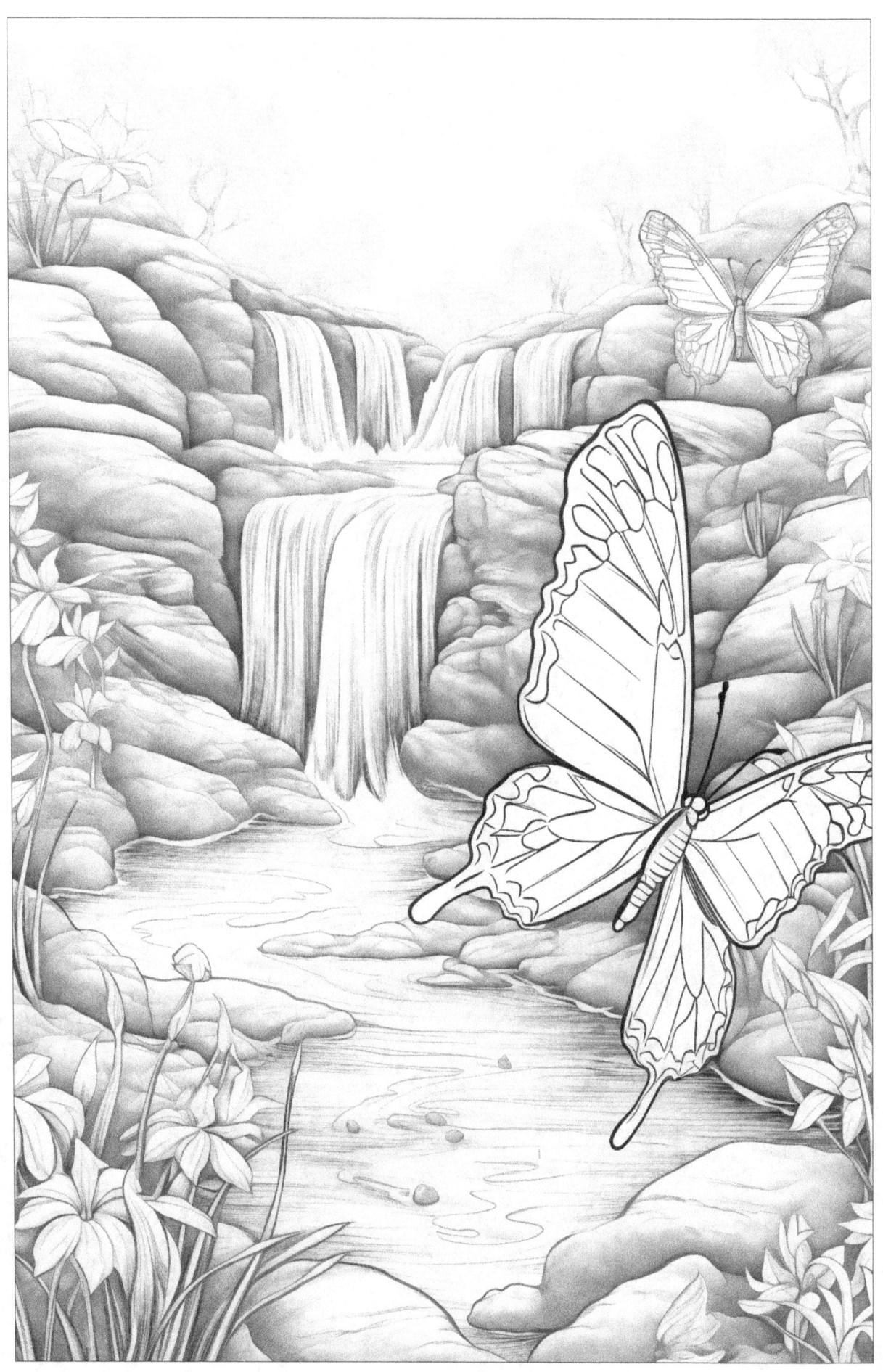

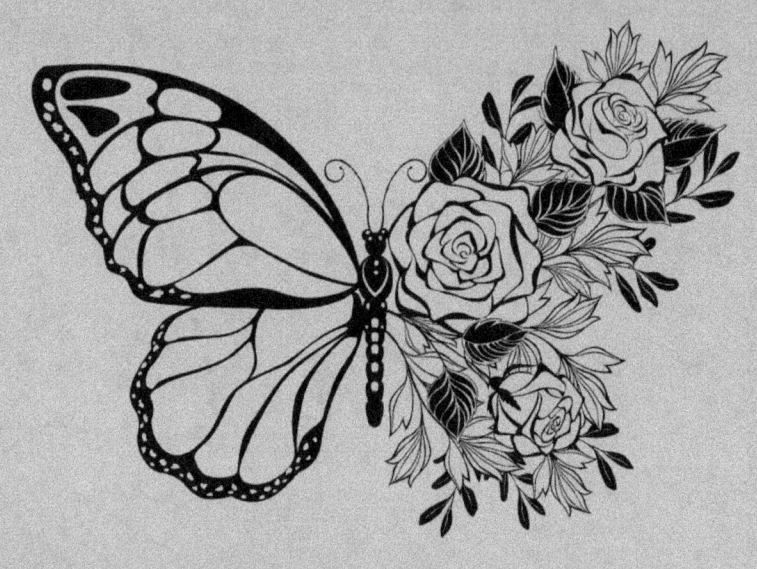

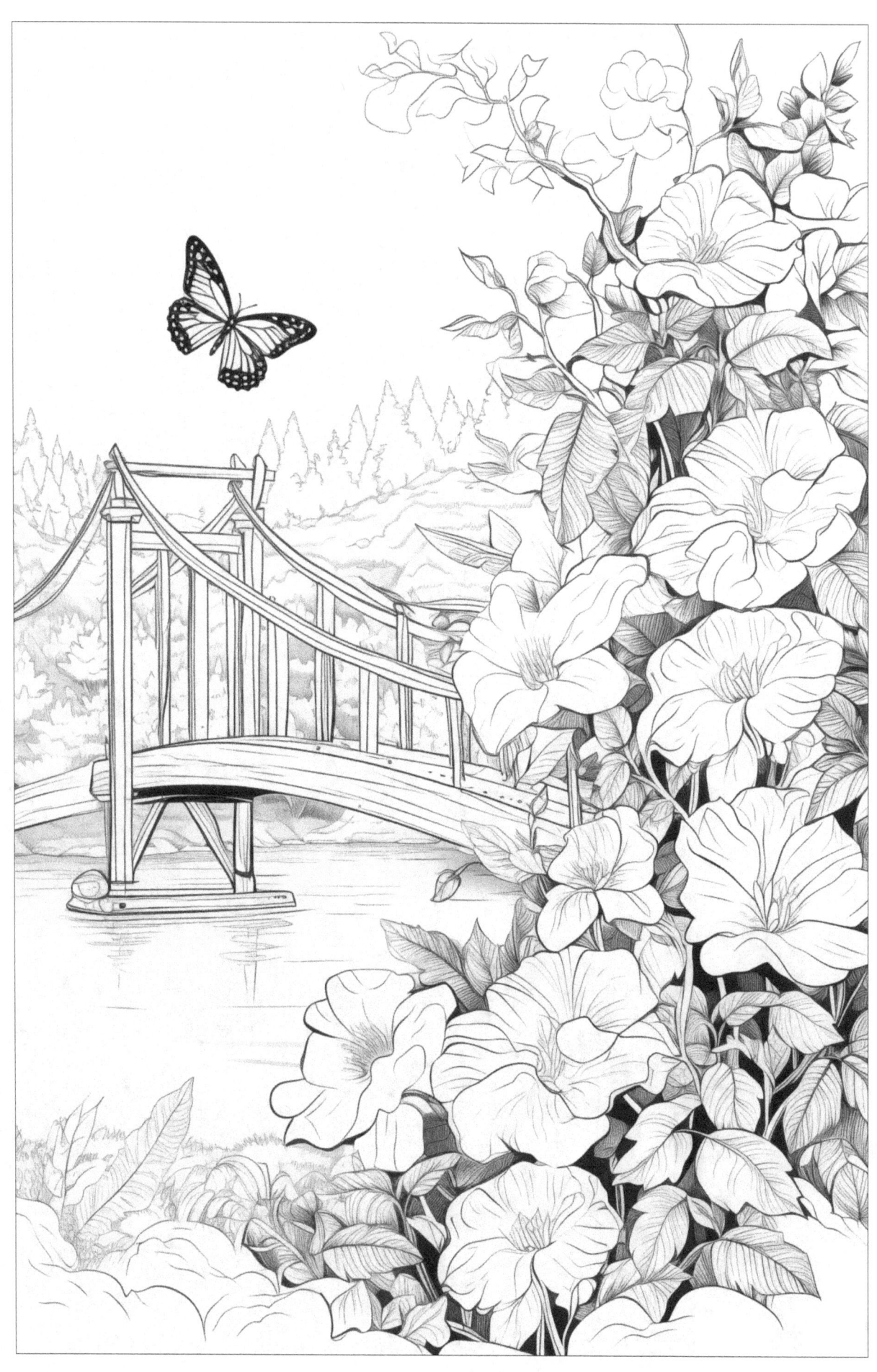

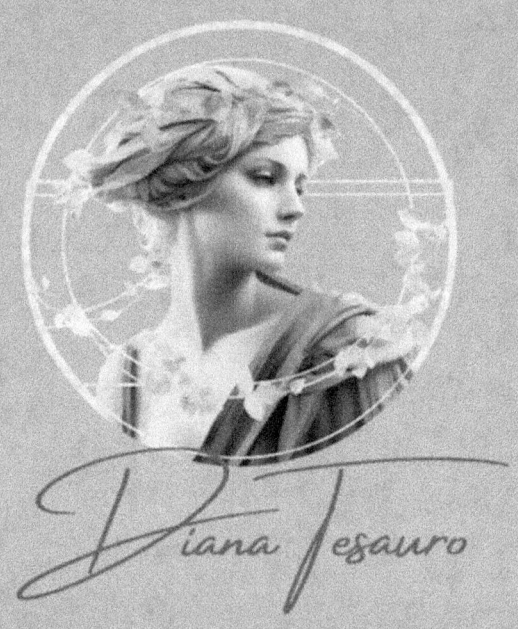

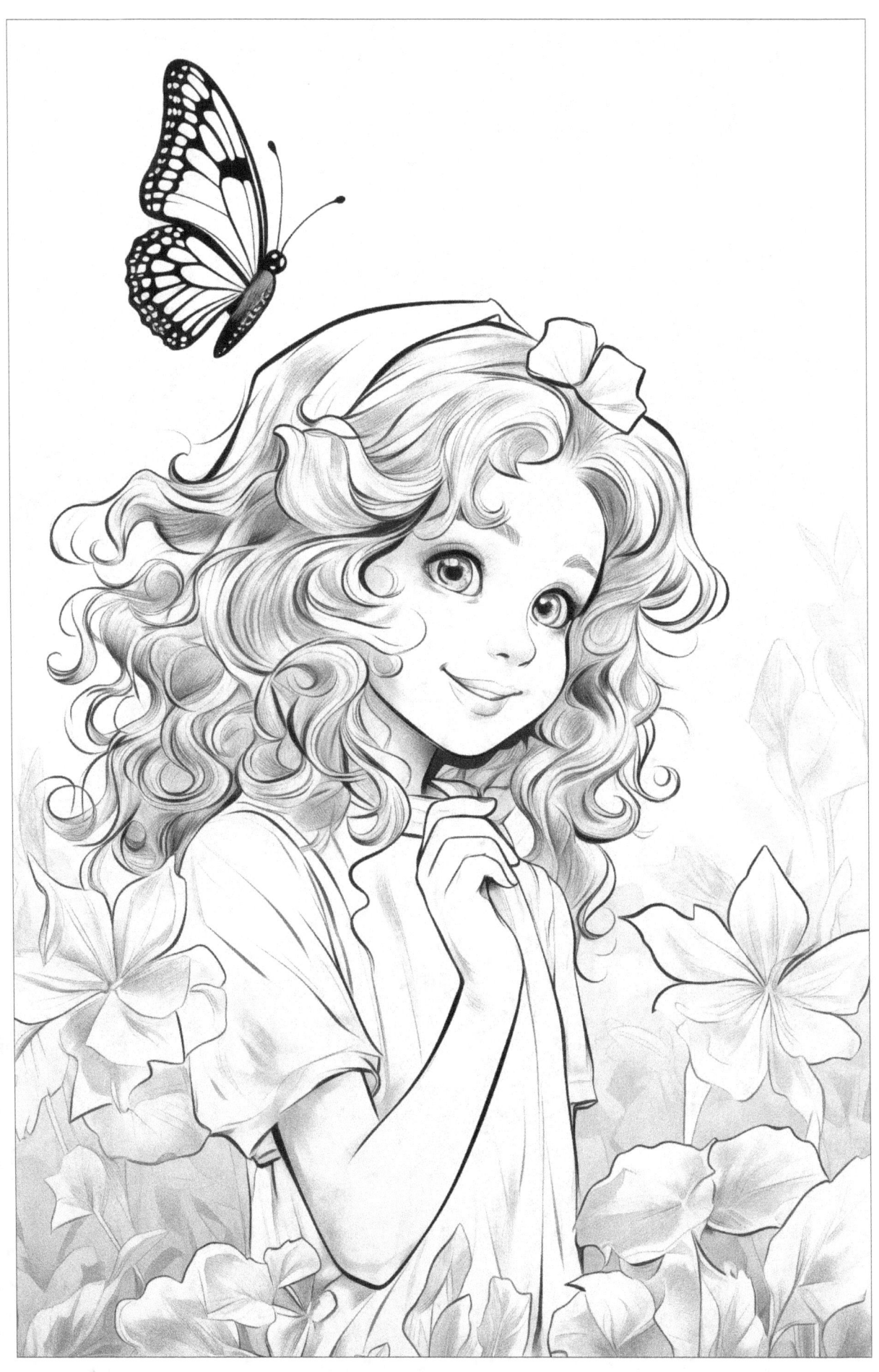

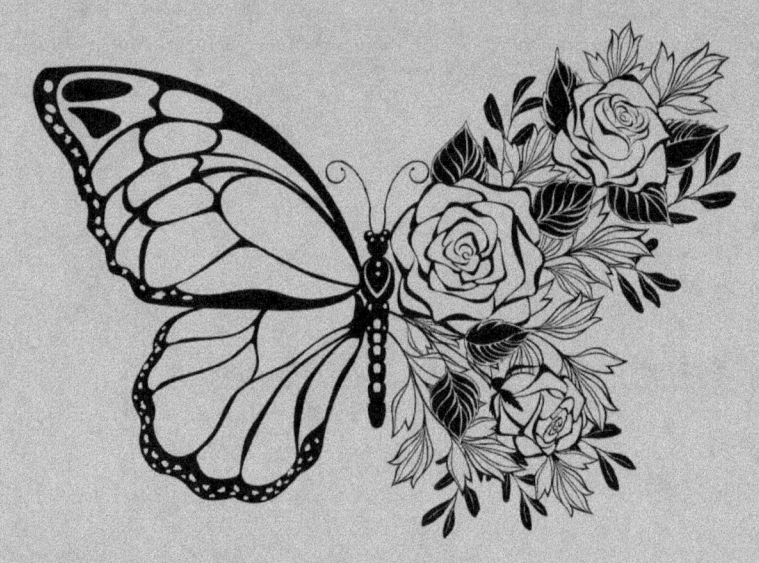

CONCLUSION

In the hope that you had fun and relaxed, I invite you to follow my profile on your preferred social channel:

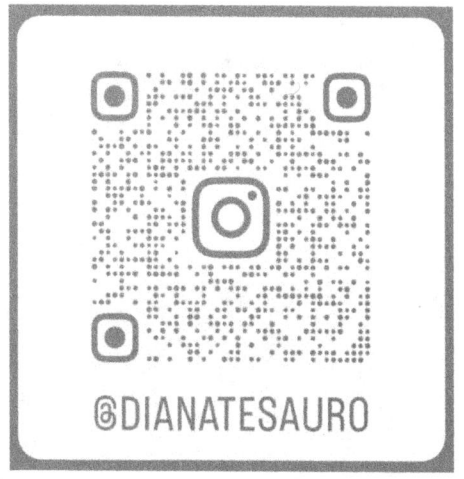

Instagram   TikTok

Stay updated and don't miss out on the upcoming releases!
Exciting new releases are on their way.

Thank you for your support.

REVIEWS ARE HELPFUL FOR AUTHORS

If you've come this far, how about taking one final step?

"Leaving a review in a store is like telling a friend that you enjoyed the book!"

Access Amazon with your account, type the book's title, click on the cover image, and leave your valuable review.

Every opinion counts and helps to grow and improve.

Thank you.

OTHER COLORING BOOKS
BY DIANA TESAURO

GREEK MYTHOLOGY | Adult coloring book

Cute and Creepy Coloring Book